D0917106

The Family and
Public Policy

THE FAMILY AND PUBLIC POLICY

The Issue of the 1980s

by
John J. Dempsey, Dr.P.H.
Policy Analyst
Office of the Assistant Secretary
for Planning and Evaluation
Office of the Secretary
U.S. Department of Health and Human Services

·P·A·U·L·H·
BROOKES
PUBLISHING Co

Baltimore • London

Paul H. Brookes Publishing Co.
Post Office Box 10624
Baltimore, Maryland 21204

Copyright 1981 by Paul H. Brookes Publishing Co., Inc.
All rights reserved.

Typeset by The Composing Room of Michigan, Inc.,
Grand Rapids, Michigan.
Manufactured in the United States of America by
Universal Lithographers, Inc., Cockeysville, Maryland.

Permission to reprint the following quotations is gratefully acknowledged:

Page 8: Quotation from Wilensky, H.L., & Lebeaux, C.N. *Industrial society and social welfare.* New York: Russell Sage Foundation, 1958, pp. 67–68. Copyright 1958 by the Russell Sage Foundation.

Pages 9 and 10: Quotations from Sussman, M.B. Family. In: John B. Turner (ed.), *Encyclopedia of Social Work, Vol. 17.* Washington, D.C.: National Association of Social Workers, 1977, pp. 357 (excerpts), 366–367 (excerpts). Copyright 1977 by the National Association of Social Workers, Inc.

Page 11: Quotations from Lasch, C. *Haven in a heartless world.* New York: Basic Books, 1977, pp. 100, 130. Copyright 1977 by Basic Books, Inc.

Page 25: Quotation from Cohen, N.E., & Connery, M.F. Government and the family. *Journal of Marriage and the Family,* 1967, *29*(1), 16–17. Copyright 1967 by the National Council on Family Relations.

Pages 30–31: Quotation from Moroney, R.M. *The family and the state: Considerations for social policy.* London: Longman Group, Ltd., 1976, pp. 138–139.

Page 32: Quotation from Kamerman, S.B. *Developing a family impact statement.* New York: Foundation for Child Development, 1976, 16–17.

Library of Congress Cataloging in Publication Data
Dempsey, John J., 1935–
 The family and public policy.

 Bibliography: p. 157
 Includes index.
 1. Family—United States—History. 2. Family policy
—United States. I. Title.
HQ535.D43 306.8'0973 81-1740
ISBN 0-933716-15-X   AACR2

Contents

Preface

Family public policy has emerged in recent years as one of the principal policy issues of these times, commanding the simultaneous attention of the political community, the professional/scientific community, and that part of the private sector that engages in political activism and policy advocacy. In my position in the federal government, I have had the privilege of witnessing the maturation of this issue, and the pages that follow are intended to share this experience, placed in historical and professional context, with readers who are interested in an overview of the scope and current nature of contemporary family policy.

I am indebted to my superiors in my present position for their support of my interest in family public policy. I am indebted to all those who participated in the 1980 White House Conference on Families—a remarkable assemblage of family members, Congressmen, religious and business leaders, professionals, and representatives of activist groups, all of whom were inspiring in their commitments to the American family. I am also indebted to those who critiqued early drafts of this manuscript; I particularly want to acknowledge the advice of Marvin Sussman of the University of Delaware, Roger White of Johns Hopkins University, John Carr of the White House Conference on Families, and Edwin Marcus of the U.S. Department of Health and Human Services.

The opinions expressed herein are strictly my own, and do not necessarily agree or conflict with the opinions of any other official in the federal government.

Introduction

Over the past 25 years there has been a progressive interest in both the political and the professional/scientific communities in the impact of governmental action on the well-being of American families. Early rhetoric has been displaced by serious consideration among policymakers, and several very recent calls to action have created a policy climate that many feel will make the family THE policy issue of the 1980s.

This book is a chronicle of the emergence of the family as a public policy issue. It traces the changes in the family from the colonial period on, the maturation of professional and scientific interest in the family, the evolution of public uncertainties about the potential of implemented policy, the progressive involvement of the political and scientific communities in substantive family issues, the development of immensely intense commitments from the 1980 White House Conference on Families, the formulation of modes of conceptualizing problems and policy responses, and the crystallization of some hard choices in the years ahead. Therefore, the book is characterized by its breadth of scope rather than by an in-depth study of the family and its problems or by a detailed analysis of the public policy process.

Although public policy is formulated at every level of government, nearly all attention is limited here to public policy at the national level. This is an extension of an earlier interest (Dempsey, 1975) in the consumer-provider relationship in regard to families with handicapped children, in which the quality of the child's development was conceptualized as the outcome of the consumer-provider relationship, as the outcome of the quality of the division of labor formed between families and professionals. Since federal government influence on both the consumer and the provider side of the equation has expanded markedly, it is both logical and timely to expand that interest to the more general contemporary issue of families and public policy.

Despite the universal reverence in which the family is held, opinions vary on its strengths and weaknesses, and feelings run high on the nature of the federal government's relationship to it. The contemporary debate on family policy, therefore, is lively, important, and likely to occupy center stage in the public's attention for quite some time. This book is intended to introduce the reader to the dimensions of the contemporary scene.

The Family and
Public Policy

Chapter 1

Historical Perspectives

Recent interest in family public policy did not originate spontaneously, but was a logical outgrowth of several historical processes that converged after World War II. These include changes in the role of the traditional American family, industrialization and urbanization, the secularization of society and the growth of family-relevant professions and sciences, the centralization of government, and the declining view of the competence of technologists in the eyes of the public. This chapter identifies these historical processes and leads into Chapter 2, which concentrates solely on the emergence of interest in family public policy.

THE COLONIAL FAMILY HERITAGE

Modern education has been criticized for many shortcomings, but no one has challenged its consistently effective job of providing each new generation of children with a reverent predisposition toward our founders. We seem to have an insatiable appetite for anything that extols the triumphs of our forefathers or charts our growth from primitive settlements to world power.

The early colonial societies were, of course, principally agrarian and the family was the omnibus institution of those times. Families in isolated settlements were of necessity largely responsible for their housing, food, recreation and entertainment, the education and moral upbringing of their children, income-producing products, defense, and the care of ailing members. It was a harsh life, marred by crop failures, Indian and other wars, physical discomfort, and high mortality for every age group. It was also simple and rewarding in ways many contemporary people have come to envy and glorify.

Supports for family life were principally drawn from its members. The large, extended family was the preferred type since many people were needed to assume a flexible division of labor to carry out all the functions necessary for survival, security, and a full life. Neighboring families routinely supported each other in construction, planting and harvesting, recreation, defense, crisis

1

management, and other areas requiring collective action. The church provided spiritual stimulation, general guidance and support, and consolation in bad times. Since so many of life's tragedies were beyond the *control* of families, the church provided a constructive, *accepting* philosophy that reinterpreted calamities as part of the divine scheme and, consequently, as an opportunity for spiritual growth.

This notion of control is central to an understanding of changes in family life that have recently elevated the issue of family policy to prominence. Compared to today, relatively few controls over life existed in colonial times, mainly because of the undeveloped state of technology at that time. Women died in labor of easily corrected complications and men went blind of simply treated infections. Crops failed because of treatable diseases and controllable pests. Emotional upheavals that could easily have been stabilized by drugs progressed to bizarre, maniacal proportions. Accessible subterranean ores went undeveloped or were mined with excruciating effort.

To be sure, the early settlers did a superb job of controlling what was to be controlled—home construction, food production, deviant behavior, security, defense, education—and the principal unit of control was the family. Yet, many of the forces affecting life were beyond control, in comparison to contemporary society. It will be argued that, over time, the capacity to control aspects of life has increased, but most of the new capacities and some of the traditional family capacities have been allocated to new, specialized institutions of society. Stated differently, the quality of family life need not be so subject to chance now, but less of it is within the direct control of families. Whether this is good or bad is a judgment for which there isn't the remotest degree of consensus, as subsequent chapters demonstrate.

["Control" is used here and throughout as a management science term rather than as a sociological one. A distinction is made in management science between "system" and "environment" based on managerial control (Goettee, 1971). The system is what the manager controls; all else is the environment. Analogously, the family's life-system is the part of life it controls; all else is its environment—mortgage rates, employment opportunities, medical costs, TV programming, government programs, and so on. Simplistically, the quality of a family's life is determined 1) by how well it manages what it controls and 2) by the net impact of malevolent and benevolent forces in the uncontrollable environment.]

INDUSTRIALIZATION AND URBANIZATION

The processes of industrialization and urbanization throughout this country's history have been well studied for their human impact (Wilensky & Lebeaux, 1958). Although the two processes are generally discussed in tandem, advances in agricultural technology as a result of industrialization have also had a profound influence on farm families, but this impact generally followed that of industrialization on urban populations.

One of the principal impacts of industrialization on urban populations was the gradual separation of home and work—first for men and later for their spouses, beginning in the nineteenth century. This reduced the scope of family interactions and the quantity of parenting. Additionally, it introduced the "money life-style"; wages from labor were used to purchase the housing, heating fuel, food, and recreation that had been produced by rural families for their own consumption. Even a temporary interruption of the flow of wages created family disasters—a common event early on, tempered more recently by labor union successes, civil service reform, and unemployment insurance. Children had been an economic asset on the farm and indispensable for old age security; in the small city dwelling, they were an economic liability and their importance for security declined with the advent of pensions and Social Security. Early attempts by some adults to turn children into economic assets were curtailed by child labor laws. The viability of, and necessity for, the three-generation family in one household waned with vocational mobility, economic security, and the rise of the nuclear family ideal. Early on, the blue collar masses in the cities lived a stark existence, yet large numbers of families fared well enough to enjoy the cultural, recreational, and educational opportunities that were concentrated in urban areas.

Early farm families were aided immeasurably by the ready availability of cheap land and an open frontier. Surplus sons could develop nearby land for their own farms or, later, move to the frontier. As the availability of land declined, increasing prices made expansion more difficult, resettlement of surplus sons less feasible, and the urban alternative more attractive. Technological advances were a two-edged sword. For those with ample farms, machinery drastically reduced back-breaking labor and improved the yield per acre. For those with small farms or farms of marginal quality, regulated compliance with technologically attainable standards spelled disaster, such as resulted from the required use of refrigerated bulk milk tanks.

At any given point in this process, especially in the early stages, farm families were generally more in control of life than most of their urban contemporaries. How much work they cared to put into the farm was up to them, as was how much the extended family cared to diversify its economic activities to buffer against uncontrolled variables, such as the vagaries of weather. The blue collar families in the cities, in contrast, were buffeted unmercifully by repeated dips in the economy, waves of immigrants who worked for subsistence wages, and periodic epidemics that threatened life itself in the smelly, crowded, unsanitary city. The progressively pluralistic urban society made collective action against undesirable influences difficult, whereas similar influences in culturally homogeneous rural areas either proved uneconomical or were greeted with variations on the tar-and-feather routine. With time, however, controls over the economy and labor unions and government economic support programs improved the lot of the urban masses, whereas price controls and costly land and inheritance taxes and agribusiness have weakened the family farm and ushered in an entirely new class of migrant farm families, whose life circumstances now are as unstable as those of urban blue collar workers a century ago. Whether life is more controllable by families now in urban or in rural areas is highly debatable, but perhaps the edge still belongs to the rural areas, especially for the proponents of the back-to-earth philosophy.

At least, many people hope that this is still true, because life in the quiet, clean, simple "country" is a fantasy cherished by urbanites and ruralites alike. This is particularly evident in the way the U.S. has traditionally handled homeless children (Kadushin, 1974, pp. 393–399). In the colonial period, homeless children were indentured with a family that would feed and clothe them, and teach them a craft or trade—in return for which the family received their labor until their twenty-first birthdays. As industrialization separated work and home, this became less feasible for the mounting numbers of homeless children, especially in urban areas. In 1849, the New York City Chief of Police estimated that street urchins numbered in the thousands. Religious and charitable societies responded by placing such children in rural areas where their labor was useful and where they would be protected from the "pernicious" influences of the city. Even today, there are annual fund-raising campaigns in cities to send poor children for a couple wholesome weeks in the country, whereas going from the country to the city tends to be limited to family shopping trips or well-chaperoned class trips or runaways seeking the anonymity of the city.

PROFESSIONALIZATION, SECULARIZATION, AND THE TECHNOCRACY: THE FIRST HALF OF THE TWENTIETH CENTURY

Surely the first half of the twentieth century will be remembered as science's finest hour. Technology progressed from the Wright brothers to jets. We witnessed the development of antibiotics, indoor plumbing, electrical gadgets, nuclear energy, rangefinder cameras, subways, skyscrapers, wrist watches, frozen vegetables, calculators, phonographs, telephones, and margarine.

The capabilities of the growing federal establishment seemed boundless. Two successful world wars proved our might. The G-men triumphed over the gangsters. The 1935 Social Security Act and post–World War II housing acts were viewed as the beginning of the end of abject human deprivation. The great depression had been solved. Expectations were high.

From humble beginnings in the nineteenth century, new professions joined the old in an impressive growth of knowledge and skills about human needs. Education for all. Dr. Spock for all. New insights into the desirability of permissive childrearing. New drugs for stabilizing mental illness. The decline of massive epidemics. Public housing. Marriage counseling. Innovations for the mentally retarded. Greater longevity. Libraries everywhere. National parks. Welfare reform. Successful labor unions. Pensions. Freud. Margaret Mead. Mayo. Mary Richmond. Talcott Parsons.

The dominant theme in all this was the growth of secularism at the expense of the theistic perception of the world. Instead of seeking hidden meaning in life's unfortunate circumstances, the new technocracy promised increasing control over life's problems. The destructive youngster wasn't sinful, he was acting out conflicts at home and at school—a treatable phenomenon. Divorce resulted from limited insight about resolvable conflicts, not from a failure to fulfill God's expectations. The birth of a crippled child was not a providential act, it was an opportunity to treat and habilitate a handicapped person. The sciences redefined human existence in natural terms for which natural solutions could be sought.

Interestingly, secularism and religion proved not to be incompatible. In the early half of the twentieth century, the leading schools of medicine, education, law, social work, and other fields were in sectarian universities, and human service innovations were frequently conducted under religious auspices. The psychologist of the 1950s did not necessarily find membership in his profession and in his church in conflict, even though his secular approach to behavior would have outraged the church 200 years earlier. Too little has been written about how well many religious groups have integrated the ever-expanding secular technology with their traditional philosophy and theology.

All in all, as the first half of the twentieth century ended, the general population was in awe of the daily advances of technology, and expectations were high for society-wide improvements through the organized efforts of both the public and private sectors.

PROFESSIONAL/SCIENTIFIC INTEREST IN THE FAMILY

Although some sciences and professions such as medicine and law originated in antiquity, most originated humbly in the nineteenth century and began to mature in the early twentieth century, such as sociology and social work. At no time in the twentieth century has there been a shortage of professional/scientific interest in the family, and the growth of this interest to the present is discussed here.

The credibility of the professions/sciences is tied to their research base, in which hypotheses are tested and yield, over time, an expanding knowledge base about reality and interventions in it. Some of the earliest researches were family oriented, but not necessarily in the finest tradition of science. Goddard's (1912) study of the Kallikak family, for instance, is a curious blend of scientific method, moral values, and primitive eugenics. It seems that there was a landed nineteenth century gentleman whose legitimate sons and their sons for several generations were staunch citizens in the highest tradition. He did have some very human moments, however, and sired children by a local woman of dubious character. This second line of descendants included a motley assortment of retarded persons, debaucherers, and ne'er-do-wells of every sort. Goddard's poorly supported association between moral behavior and IQ status was an embarrassment to researchers for quite some time.

The most extensive effort to chart the growth of professional/scientific interest in the family has been an on-going effort at the Minnesota Family Study Center (MFSC) at the University of Minnesota. This charting of the literature has been limited to the research literature of the various disciplines, but is world-wide in scope.

In August, 1980, Reuben Hill reported an analysis of the MFSC's inventory from 1900 on. The total world output of scholarly books and journals has been over 25,000—two-thirds in English. Most of the scientifically acceptable work has been published since the end of World War II, and presently the annual outpouring of publications is in excess of 2000—a volume well beyond the ability of any single scholar.

Inspection of Table 1 reveals several trends in family research so far in this century. Some family topics have enjoyed a relatively stable interest, in terms of proportion of total interest, such as "Family Transactions with Groups and Organizations." Some family topics have declined in interest, such as "Marriage and Divorce," and some topics have received increasing attention, such as "Surveys of Institutional Aids to Families," which includes marriage counseling and marriage preparation programs as well as the impact of national policies and programs—the subject of this book.

New issues were added to the MFSC inventory in the 1970s, with "Family, Work, and Economy" receiving the most attention.

In terms of family public policy, the early literature was entirely European, according to Hill. Although some policy writing appeared as early as 1948 in *Marriage and Family Living* and the *American Journal of Sociology*, the first continuous thread of interest did not appear until the 1965–1972 period, during which the U.S. contributed 50% of the world literature. Although the number of journals publishing family research has recently approached 800, the first journal to specialize in family public policy has not yet made its debut. (A sample of this literature on family policy is discussed in Chapter 2.)

Even the finest family research suffers from the fact that it is conducted by humans. Hill offers a list of topics about which research has generated conflicting results, which includes the following propositions (p. 230):

The economic factor is not significant in divorce or marriage adjustment. Children in a family lower its vulnerability to divorce.

Table 1. Proportion of family research references by subject matter categories, 1900–78[a]

	1900–44	45–53	54–59	60–64	65–68	69–72	73–74	75–76	77–78	Total 1900–78 No.	%
Macroscopic Studies	17.2	13.7	18.6	16.4	9.9	9.2	8.3	6.4	8.6	4460	11.8
Family Transactions with Groups & Organizations	15.5	17.3	17.8	16.4	16.7	15.9	16.9	17.4	16.3	6276	16.6
Family as Small Group	17.7	21.4	23.2	23.9	22.3	25.3	22.0	21.7	20.4	8329	22.1
Mate Selection	3.1	3.7	2.7	3.0	2.1	2.3	1.6	1.4	1.6	855	2.3
Marriage & Divorce	14.4	12.2	10.8	8.0	5.9	6.3	4.0	3.8	5.1	2873	7.6
Family Reproduction Behavior	9.2	6.3	6.1	6.4	10.1	8.3	11.5	11.8	9.6	3337	8.8
Man & Sexual Behavior	2.8	2.2	1.7	2.0	3.1	2.4	3.5	3.2	4.6	1118	3.0
Families with Special Problems	10.3	9.2	9.6	11.0	13.8	16.2	13.9	14.5	13.0	4776	12.7
Minority Groups	4.1	3.0	2.7	3.2	3.2	3.0	4.2	3.0	2.8	1206	3.2
Surveys of Institutional Aids to Families	2.0	4.8	2.6	4.2	5.8	3.0	8.0	11.3	10.3	2230	5.9
Assessments of Family Research	2.2	4.7	3.7	4.5	6.3	7.7	6.1	5.5	7.7	2115	5.6
Other	1.5	1.5	0.5	0.6	0.7	0.4	0.0	0.0	0.0	176	0.4
Total	100.0	100.0	100.0	100.0	100.0	100.0	100.0	100.0	100.0	37751	100.0
Total Number of Publications	2714	2526	3682	4939	4364	4494	3502	3099	3216		

Sources: Volumes I–V of the Minnesota Inventories; Aldous-Hill (1969); Aldous-Dahl (1974); Olson-Dahl (1975, 1977); Olson (1979).

[a]This table appears as Exhibit 8.5 in Hill (1980), p. 200.

Adolescents look more to their peers than to their parents for their values and standards.

Fathers are of diminishing functional importance to the personality development of children.

Urban middle class families are isolated and insulated from kinsmen and supporting social networks.

Of the many conclusions that can be drawn from Hill's work, three seem particularly relevant here:

1. His data prove incontrovertibly that the volume of interest in the family within the professional/scientific community has been immense in the twentieth century and is increasing.
2. Interest in public policy, although of recent vintage, is increasing.
3. Although the growth in substantive knowledge about the family has been impressive, there are many important, extensively studied topics for which there is no scientific consensus.

In addition to the specific debatable issues above is the more general one of the total impact of a changing, industrializing society on the family. Two different views of this are highlighted by Wilensky and Lebeaux (1958, pp. 67–68):

> Popular discussion reveals two dominant views as to what is happening to the American family. Family expert Carle C. Zimmerman, a proponent of one view, says the family is dissolving. Divorce is on the increase; more wives are working and therefore spend less time with the family; the marriage contract is becoming less sacred and more secular; parents are losing authority over children (a fact seen in the "revolt of youth"). Above all, an "unbridled individualism" and a decline in the spirit of self-sacrifice have led to a decline in the birth rate; women are now less willing to bear the large broods of children who form the basis of familism. The decay of the family, our most important primary group, heralds the further decay of civilization itself.
>
> The second view—early stated by another family expert, Joseph K. Folsom—holds that the family is simply changing its organization, and will emerge strengthened, better adapted to a democratic society. The double standard in sex is declining; choice of mate is more voluntary; mechanization of the smaller home plus a flood of goods and services have reduced the drudgery of housework; males are less dominant, wives have more equality in law and in daily living (liberalization of divorce and decline of church authority make it easier to get rid of a cruel husband). Above all, there is a partial shift of traditional family functions—protective, educational, economic—to the state, school, and industry. This makes family members more independent of one another. It thereby strengthens the family as an adaptable emotional unit. Love, freed from economic compulsion and parental authority, may become more loyal and permanent. Companionship and satisfying affection in the family will create men who are less inclined to sabotage democracy in the community.

Each science/profession approaches the family from a different perspective. The following sections on these perspectives are intended more to illustrate the variety of interests in, and approaches to, the family than to explore any given perspective in depth.

Sociology

Perhaps no other discipline has been so intimately involved in family matters as sociology. Courses in the family are commonplace in undergraduate sequences. The value of sociological work on many theoretical and empirical issues nearly dominates the literature and has substantially influenced professions such as social work and psychiatry. References throughout these pages are drawn more from sociology than from any other single source.

Sussman (1977) offers the following general description of family functions:

> The family is a universal concept, not only for man but for all species in all times. For Homo sapiens, the family is a group of individuals in interaction. . . .
>
> The family functions as a facilitating, mediating, and confronting system for its members who have different aspirations, capabilities, and potential. Families adapt to urban or industrial life and simultaneously influence the development, structure, and activities of the contemporary social institutions and organizations. Largely because of variations in family structure and the life cycle, families differ in how well they adapt to the complexities of modern life, their efforts to mitigate the demands of nonfamily groups, and their ability to influence the behavior of outside organizations such as the school, social welfare agency, or factory. Consequently, the main tasks of families are to develop their capacities to socialize children, to enhance and facilitate the competence of their members to cope with the demands of other organizations in which they must function, to use these organizations for the benefits they provide, and to provide for their members' satisfactions and a mentally and physically healthy environment that is intrinsic to the well-being of the family.

Variations in family type have interested sociologists in recent years, and Sussman estimates the proportion of each type in the U.S. population (personal communication):

Traditional forms of the family	
Nuclear intact family—husband, wife, and off-spring in an intact household	28%
Nuclear dyad—husband and wife living alone, childless or with no children at home	13
Nuclear remarried family—husband, wife, and off-spring of this or previous marriages living in a common household	15
Single-parent family—one head, as a consequence of divorce, abandonment, or separation, and usually including preschool and/or school-age children	18
Kin network—three-generation or extended families; members may live in same household or in close geographical proximity and operate in a reciprocal system of exchange of goods and services	4

Single and relative families—composed of single,
widowed, separated, or divorced relatives living
as single persons in households or groups   17
Emerging experimental forms
Commune family—either monogamous or group
marriage
Unmarried parent and child—usually a never-
married mother and child   5
Unmarried couple and child—usually a common-
law marriage   100%

One of the interesting debates in sociology centers on the kinship net-works of families—their current strength and their potential. Sussman, more than many others, holds the potential of family support systems highly (1977, p. 367):

Complex societies traditionally develop extensive provider systems to help meet the social, welfare, leisure, and health needs of the population. In so doing, they create bureaucratic systems to provide centralized and professionalized services. However, as services and the population increase, skyrocketing costs for services threaten the society's economy and its ability to maintain existing services or to provide new services for real or derived needs. Thus, especially since the 1960s, the unchecked use of a society's resources for the provision of such services has been questioned, as well as the issue of whether societies have reached their capacity to provide various kinds of services. Consequently there is interest in alternative, less costly systems for meeting the needs of dependent populations.

One approach is to examine the extent to which family networks might be able to provide such care, particularly if resources are made available to them. The task is to work out incentive systems so that member units of family networks can absorb such responsibilities without reducing their options or failing to reach their goals of maintaining a certain quality of life. More research is needed to develop appropriate financial and service supports to enable the family to provide a creative environment for its dependent members and to do so at less cost than existing alternatives.

History

It comes as a surprise to many to find that historians have had a considerable amount of interest in families—not the elite families of royalty nor the families of industrial tycoons and celebrated leaders, but the average families that comprise society. The volume of interest has progressed to the point that the *Journal of Family History* has made its debut in recent years.

Among the more controversial recent works is historian Christopher Lasch's *Haven in a Heartless World* (1977). His initial consideration of the history of the family shifts quickly to the history of professional thought on family life and professional influence on it. His conclusions are not always complimentary.

In the context of a shift of family functions to society's institutions over time, Lasch also sees a shift in authority from religion to law to science. He identifies psychiatrist Harry Stack Sullivan as one of those who accorded a lofty responsibility for social control to psychiatrists, who thus become "doctors to a sick society":

> Educators and psychiatrists, [Sullivan] wrote, had to assume the burdens of parenthood, so wretchedly performed by most parents. "Parents must be made to see that children are in no sense their chattels but instead their wards, held in trust as future members of the community." The "helping professions" had long demanded greater control over socialization, but they had never before won such widespread approval for their program. Nor had they drawn such explicit analogies between social engineering and preventive medicine. The prestige of the psychiatric profession, the growing domination of psychiatric points of view in social work and marriage counseling, and the growing belief among liberals that war and class conflict originated in the "authoritarian personality" created a cultural climate highly receptive to medical modes of thought. Enlightened opinion now identified itself with the medicalization of society: the substitution of medical and psychiatric authority for the authority of parents, priests, and law-givers, now condemned as representatives of discredited authoritarian modes of discipline.

Again in the context of the loss of family functions to social institutions, Lasch offers the following critique of sociologist Talcott Parsons:

> When a theory is open to so many empirical objections, we begin to suspect that there is something wrong with the theory itself. Parsons's theory of the family rests on an unwarranted assumption which he took from his predecessors and never subjected to critical analysis: that some of the family's functions can be surrendered without weakening the others. In fact, the so-called functions of the family form an integrated system. It is inaccurate to speak of a variety of functions, some of which decline while others take on added importance. The only function of the family that matters is socialization; and when protection, work, and instruction in work have all been removed from the home, the child no longer identifies with his parents or internalizes their authority in the same way as before.

Lasch, probably more so than any other single contemporary writer, postulates that the increasing prominence of scientific experts in society is predictable and perhaps inevitable, but also potentially dangerous.

Economics

Although economics has traditionally concentrated on markets and exchange, economic theory recently has been found to be applicable to processes *within* the family. Sawhill (1977) states:

> There are several reasons for the economist's newly discovered interest in the family. One stems from the common views of most economists and their own definition of the scope of their discipline, the core of which is that an economic problem exists whenever resources that have multiple and competing uses are scarce. Scarcity requires *choice,* and choices are best guided by comparing the costs and benefits of all the possible alternatives. Once one has defined "re-

sources'' and ''costs and benefits'' broadly enough, there is almost no area of human behavior to which the economic paradigm cannot be applied.

Since resources include human resources and time, and since individuals are ''rational''—they choose alternatives that maximize their welfare—they are faced with decisions about whether to marry (when and to whom), who should work and how much, whether to have children, and so on:

> All the above decisions are influenced by the costs and benefits associated with the various alternatives. Costs are measured in both time and money and include psychic elements as well as opportunities foregone (e.g., one of the costs of marrying individual A is not marrying individual B). Similarly, benefits may be monetary or non-monetary in character (e.g., if a woman quits her job to keep house, it is because her time at home is valued more than the income she would have earned). Thus, the broad applicability of economic theory to a wide range of nonmarket phenomena is one reason for the economist's emerging interest in the family. (Sawhill, 1977)

Social Work

Social work has probably been more continuously family oriented than any other profession. It traces its origins to the Charity Organization Societies of the late nineteenth century, which relied mainly on well-intentioned, but poorly trained, volunteers. In 1919, the new American Association for Organizing Family Social Work assumed a dominant role in the profession, and later Mary Richmond's ''social diagnosis'' provided the skeleton for the profession's knowledge base, with a pervasive orientation to the family as a unit of conceptualization and service.

The Family Service Association of America has been the principal standard setter for family social work for many decades. It consists of several hundred affiliated agencies with over 4000 trained staff members, serving a half million families per year. They provide family counseling, adoption services, foster care, consultation to community agencies, and a host of specialized programs that vary from community to community.

Social work is probably more dependent on public policy for its self-expression than any other profession. Only a small percentage of its members are in private practice, and private practice at all is relatively new. Most social workers are salaried in organizations, with government-supported programs increasingly dominant. Policy recommendations have emanated from the National Association of Social Workers for decades.

The knowledge base of social work is eclectic. In its early days it borrowed heavily from psychiatry, but sociology gained much prominence in the 1950s and many recent social work publications may be called ''applied sociology,'' in reflection of the rather homogeneous social science knowledge base in them.

In addition to the continuing refinement of family treatment models (Mostwin, 1980), the profession has increasingly invested itself in political activism for various public policy reforms, which are discussed in several sections of subsequent chapters.

In contrast to the general family service agency, many social workers are employed in multidisciplinary settings such as hospitals, courts, community mental health centers, public housing authorities, and other settings; the family dimension is one of the principal contributions in these settings, in activities ranging from case management to broad social planning.

Law

Since public policy always involves law, the lawyer is a *sine qua non* among public policy professionals. More specific to this book, for some of the more unfortunate family events—divorce, abuse, child neglect—family members may secure the services of private attorneys or come before a judge or magistrate in a family court.

"Family law" generically refers to the latter, and is becoming a major area of specialization, having its own section in the American Bar Association and its own journal, *Family Law Quarterly*. The entire October, 1977, issue of *The Family Coordinator* is devoted to the many facets of family law; Henley, in that issue, lists 26 topics that are keys to its mushrooming literature:

General
Abortion
Adoption
Alimony
Child abuse and neglect
Child custody
Child support
Children and the law
Divorce
Education
Equal rights
Family courts and counseling
Foster care
Inheritance
Intrafamily immunity
Juvenile delinquency
Marriage
Medico-legal problems
Mental competence
Parental rights and responsibilities
Privacy
Property

Regulation of conception
Sexuality issues
Taxes
Unwed parents and illegitimate children

Psychiatry and Psychology

Since much human mental pathology originates in destructive interrelationships in the family, psychotherapists—particularly psychiatrists and clinical
psychologists—have traditionally placed therapy in a family context. Ackerman (1958) identifies many of the dimensions of this context:

> This approach attempts to correlate the dynamic psychological processes of indi-
> vidual behavior with family behavior in order to be able to place individual
> clinical diagnosis and therapy within the broader frame of family diagnosis and
> therapy. It has been necessary, therefore, to explore a series of interrelated
> themes: the interdependence of individual and family stability at every stage of
> growth from infancy to old age; the role of the family in the emotional develop-
> ment of the child; the family as stabilizer of the mental health of the adult; the
> family as conveyer belt for anxiety and conflict and as a carrier of the contagion
> of mental illness; the interplay of conflict between family and community, con-
> flict in family relationships, and conflict within individual family members; and
> breakdown in adaptation and illness as symptoms of the group pathology of the
> family.

Religion

Religion is not a profession or science in the secular sense because its base is
divine revelation rather than the scientific method, yet its interest in the family
has been so continuous that it cannot be ignored here. Beyond its traditional
interest in family events from birth through marriage to burial, religion is
relevant to our considerations here in at least three ways. First, it has sponsored elements of the secular service system such as hospitals, social agencies, professional schools, recreation centers, and homes for the elderly.
Second, there has been an upswing in political activism among religious
groups, which is further discussed in Chapter 4. Third, there has been an
upswing in interest in family ministry in several religions in recent years. The
Catholic Church, for instance, sponsored several activities in the 1970s that
revealed such an intense interest in the family that 1980 was officially designated the Year of the Family and the 1980s have been designated the Decade
of the Family (*A Call to Action,* n.d.; *A Vision and Strategy,* 1978).

Consequently, religion cannot be omitted from a consideration of family
public policy since religious groups are playing an increasing role in policy
development and since family-centered religious services and activities are
part of the societal impact to which public policy contributes.

Other and Cross-cutting Interests in the Family

The set of brief profiles above is by no means exhaustive, neglecting entirely home economics, medicine, anthropology, nutrition, housing, and a host of other specialized fields relevant to the family. Detailed profiles on the complete set would constitute a book unto themselves, and perhaps such a book is long overdue.

Although each science/profession/field of endeavor has its own distinct perspective, they have much in common, especially a fascination with data. The advent of inexpensive automated data processing in recent years has expanded the opportunity for research, and few have been able to resist.

The most recent data compilation at hand is from Snapper (August, 1980); the following is a very small selection of his sample. Divorce rates for first marriages have climbed steadily over the century with a dip in the depression years of the 1930s, a sharp but temporary rise following World War II, and a tendency toward leveling off since 1975. Female-headed households, as a percentage of all households, have increased during the 1970s, especially among blacks and hispanic families. Median family income in 1978 was $18,368 for white families, $12,566 for families of hispanic descent, and $11,754 for black families. In terms of the poverty level, family size and ethnicity are relevant; of families with seven or more persons, 15.7% of white, 41.3% of black, and 35.5% of hispanic families were below the poverty level in 1979. "The greatest over-representation of families below the poverty level is for black female households in which no spouse is present. Bureau of the Census data indicate that there was a 50% increase (from 740,000 to 1.2 million) in the number of such families between 1969 and 1977" (Snapper, 1980, p. 121). More and more women are working; women in the labor force as a percentage of the total labor force started at 18.1% in 1900 and progressively increased to 24.6% in 1940, 32.3% in 1960, and 41.2% in 1979. Women's earnings, as a percentage of men's earnings, have remained at 61–62% for the past decade. Mortality rates have fallen over the century and most persons have good health; 14% of all persons, however, report some limitation of activity.

In general, the unmistakable conclusion from all of the above is that the family has never suffered from lack of professional/scientific interest at any time in this century in terms of study or service. An expanding knowledge base and an improving technology leave the set of sciences/professions progressively more able to understand the family and to render potentially effective services to it.

THE TARNISHED IMAGE

Unfortunately, the reputations of the professions/sciences/service systems have not kept pace with their ever-expanding competence. As the first half of the twentieth century had been an era of glorifying science, the professions, and government, the second half has thus far witnessed the tarnishing of that image.

Some of the sharpest criticism has emanated from the ranks. Senator Proxmire, for instance, gained considerable attention for his Golden Fleece Award for the bureaucratic blunder of the month. More subtly, however, the professions received their most substantive criticism from within. Eli Bower (1960), for instance, prefaced his book on emotionally handicapped children with the following unusual story:

> Luther Woodward, at a meeting of the American Orthopsychiatric Association, described an ancient Cornish test of insanity as follows: The subject to be tested was placed in a room in which there was a pail of water directly under a water faucet. The water was turned on and the subject given a ladle and asked to bail the water from the pail. If he first turned off the faucet before beginning to bail, he was considered sane. If he continued to bail with the water still running into the pail, he was declared insane.

He was alluding to the neglect by professions and service systems of prevention. Virtually all the helping professions and service systems originated in response to abject human pathology. Although that was admirable, he maintained, limiting one's attention to present problems, without identifying and reducing their causes, makes as much sense as ladling out the bucket with the faucet on. Yet that is the type of service system we have. (In subsequent chapters this is referred to as Bower's bucket.)

Yet, most of the disillusionment has been in the general public. Permissive childrearing did not seem to be having the desired effect and the awesome psychiatrist became subject to "shrink" jokes. Nuclear scientists experienced a general decline in public esteem, capped by the Three Mile Island crisis. Social workers became distrusted by the poor and feared by the taxpayer. Parents of children with learning problems experienced the agony of conflicting "expert" advice. And the lofty physician fell the farthest. Rising fees and fewer home visits, incredible emergency room care, debates about the safety of diets, scandals about Medicaid and Medicare ripoffs, the discovery that all those newfangled X rays you had might cause cancer—all combined to transform reverence into malpractice suits.

Government has fared no better. From the standoff in Korea through the loss in Vietnam to the humiliation in Iran, our self-image of omnipotence was bludgeoned into sobriety. The War on Poverty was racked by scandals. The sheer weight of well-intentioned regulations became oppressive. Early public housing settlements soon resembled the slums around them. The expanding FDA list of carcinogens was greeted somberly, then questioningly, and finally jocularly. Economists in and out of government contradicted each other constantly. Scandals swept from the Oval Office to Congress and to state officials. Payroll deductions for Social Security rose to menacing levels. Newspaper accounts of government mismanagement, fraud, and ineptitude became commonplace. Many began to wonder whether *anything* was going right, and some recalled the comment by Will Rogers decades earlier that "we should be very glad we're not getting all the government we're paying for." And as we paid dearly for more and more and more federal programs, it seemed as though there were more and more and more problems. (Bower's bucket?)

In many respects this tarnishing of images has been healthy. The public's performance expectations of scientists and professionals and government had been unrealistically high, yet the adjustment of expectations to reality has not been a pleasant process for anyone. Most disturbing of all seems to be the current widespread uneasiness about how much beyond oneself one can trust. As the forces in society had become larger and more complex and beyond individual control, it had been easy to trust the "pros" to take control for us. As the pros demonstrated their humanity, however, some people experienced insecurity, some reacted with cynical detachment, some advocated looking within for solutions to life's problems, some withdrew into drugs and bizarre life-styles, and most . . . just . . . weren't . . . sure. "Something to believe in" is a human need that has been largely overlooked in the research literature.

Few people want to turn the clocks back to the colonial period when families had more direct control over basic functions; nearly all want modern education and medical care and contemporary housing. The capabilities of the specialists are improving constantly and most people recognize that they can't do as well for themselves as the specialists can in many areas, and they can't protect themselves as well without labor unions and immigration laws and various other governmental interventions. Yet too many people have had negative personal relationships with officialdom, nearly everyone has witnessed the defrocking of organized society in the media, and an unknown proportion see the expansion of official effort to an effective level as beyond our collective means. It is an uneasy blend of necessary dependence, fallen heroes, and limited resources. The *capacity* for a great society still seems to be cherished, but . . . there . . . are . . . doubts.

It is in this context that interest in family policy made its debut.

Chapter 2

The Emergence of Interest in Family Public Policy

For something that has become a national issue of intense and widespread interest, "family public policy" has had a very short history in the United States—15 years at this writing. Since "where we are" relative to family public policy is aided by an understanding of "how we got here," this chapter is devoted to tracing the evolution of family public policy consideration from its humble origins in the mid-1960s to its uncertain, but more mature, status at the end of the 1970s.

HISTORICAL UNDERPINNINGS OF PUBLIC AND FAMILY POLICY

Industrious self-sufficiency was probably the most valued characteristic of life in the earliest days of American colonization and it has continuously occupied a high status throughout our history. Its opposite, dependent destitution, was the principal social problem in those times, and responses to it were deeply rooted in English tradition and law (Friedlander & Apte, 1980).

The foundations of Elizabethan poor law in England rested on a distinction between the worthy and unworthy poor. The worthy poor were virtuous persons whose unfortunate circumstances in life were beyond their control—widows, orphans, the infirm. The unworthy poor were worthless individuals whose problems were attributable to laziness, profligacy, or other sinful life-styles. Public responses to the worthy poor were generally adequate to sustain life, but were seldom bountiful or compassionate; the responses to the unworthy poor were consistently punitive, frequently involving imprisonment, corporal punishment, or forced labor.

In the earliest days of the colonies, this tradition was brought to bear in very personal ways on the destitute. Families were expected to take care of their unfortunate members and, barring that, solutions frequently were found at town meetings. A destitute widow might be given first pick of the fallen firewood in the town square; a blind and ailing man might be boarded with a willing family that received small amounts of in-kind (material) relief or cash subsidies to defray costs. Less worthy types might be expelled or whipped or pressed into various forms of forced labor. The earliest legislation on destitution reflected a very simple philosophy that was unencumbered by expert testimony, supportive data, or minority reports; the Virginia Poor Law Act in the early 1600s attempted to "provide work for those who could work, relief for those who could not and punishment for those who would not" (Jernegan, 1931, p. 177).

As communities grew, and, with them, the size of the problem, first parish selectmen and later overseers of the poor handled individual cases in whatever manner seemed best. As the magnitude of the problems continued to grow with time, omnibus institutions such as almshouses and poorhouses "served" a wide assortment of debtors, beggars, vagabonds, loiterers, drunks, nuisances, and ladies of the night. Again with time, these omnibus institutions were reformed into the specialized institutions that we still have for criminals, the physically handicapped, the mentally ill, the mentally retarded, and the aged. In the process, some specialized institutions have nearly disappeared—for example, homes for unwed mothers, orphanages, and tuberculosis hospitals.

Innovations in publicly supported service systems generally began in municipalities, usually in response to calamities or to problems that had grown to proportions that could not be ignored. The first health department in the country, for instance, was created in Baltimore in the 1790s; its principal function was to barricade the road to Philadelphia to keep out travelers from that city during a series of smallpox outbreaks there. State-level systems grew more slowly and did not assume a dominant role until well into this century. Dominant federal involvement in matters pertaining to human health and well-being did not flourish until the Social Security Act of 1935, in response to the Great Depression, and the massive social and health legislation of the 1960s grew in response to mounting urban unrest about neglected problems.

The change over three centuries has been so profound as to be virtually incomprehensible. The 1680 widow without family had her plight debated at the town meeting and may have received a little firewood or some discarded clothes or a room in the back of some compassionate neighbor's home. The 1980 widow without family probably receives Social Security benefits and possibly some of her husband's pension. If she is a young widow, she may be employable since the employability of women has improved dramatically. If she is an elderly widow, her medical expenses are probably covered by Medicare. Over 300 years, the status of widowhood has changed dramatically, as has the manner of government response, the extent of government response, and the level at which responsive policies have originated. So also with other forms of human need.

"Public policy" was not a topic of scientific interest until this century and has become an obsession only over the past three decades. An inspection of the card catalogue system at the Library of Congress—probably the most exhaustive title catalogue in existence—reveals a relatively small book literature on public policy before 1950, with most of that focused on the experiences of other countries (especially England and other European countries) and most of the United States literature focused on such matters as foreign policy and industrial regulation rather than human need policies. Furthermore, both the U.S. and international book literatures were and are overwhelmingly focused on national public policy rather than policy for smaller units of government. Clearly this reflects the earlier experience of foreign countries with centralized government and the earlier experience of those countries with national social programs.

Obviously, interest in public policy has always been present implicitly. Until recent decades, however, it has been simply a general interest in the way the collective will of the people manifests itself through the political system. Recent explicit interest in public policy—especially social policy—however, seems dominated by sciences/professions that are interested in positive social change and, accordingly, want to understand public policy in a way that improves 1) the effectiveness of their inputs to the policy formation process and 2) their capacity to assess the implementation of public policy. Put differently, it is not a political science literature intended to understand the policy system; it is an action literature intended to improve participation in policy formation and policy evaluation. As the role of the federal government has increased, so has its importance for study; and as the sciences/professions capable of analyzing it are increasingly supported by the federal government, it seems quite understandable that policy analysis should be blossoming into a new national pastime.

The family public policy literature has generally followed these trends. The first major book on the topic, which was widely quoted in the early American literature, was Myrdal's *Nation and the Family,* published in 1941 on the Swedish experience. In the context of rapidly falling fertility rates and the potential for a sharply declining population size, the strong central Swedish government in 1934 began a series of systematic efforts to understand the phenomenon, to set goals, and to initiate ways of attaining them. For reasons that are somewhat obscure, they intimately linked population policy with family policy from the beginning.

Myrdal (pp. 100–101) states that Swedish policy development was facilitated by a close working relationship between the political community and social scientists that allowed a blending of knowledge and values. The population and family goals that resulted included:

Increased fertility
Medium-sized families
Reproductive quality
Reduced illegitimacy
Voluntary parenthood

The means (activities—see goal attainment model in Chapter 6) to attain them included:

Family education
Birth control education
Eugenics
Prenatal care
Encouraging marriages
Relieving insecurity
Protecting working mothers
Relieving the burden of mothers
Family recreation
Redistributing income by family size
Socialization of children

Myrdal's now classic book can be approached from many perspectives. It is a good piece of policy analysis and will assume more and more historical significance with time; it was reprinted by the M.I.T. Press after World War II and warrants reprinting again in the near future. The prime reaction here, however, is that the "Swedish experiment," as Myrdal calls it, would have been completely impossible in the U.S. in the 1930s, or even now for that matter, because of two fundamental differences between the two societies.

First, as the centralized Swedish monarchy waned, it was replaced by a democracy which used a highly developed bureaucratic model for centralized administration and control. The country was small in size as well as population, so that centralized government was feasible, well tested, and widely accepted. The U.S., in contrast, was sprawling in size, had a large population, and had a well-tested tradition of dominant state and local government. The federal government was small and heavily invested in defense and commerce regulation. Roosevelt's idea in the 1930s that the federal government was responsible for solving the Great Depression was a novel idea at the time, the acceptance of which became the keystone for contemporary philosophies of federal social responsibility.

The second fundamental difference was that the culture of Sweden was rather homogeneous, making collective action possible without disenfranchising the values of sizable minorities. The U.S. culture was and is pluralistic, which makes collective action difficult without alienating sizable subpopulations with well-established, mutually exclusive, moral, social, and political value systems.

A proposal in the 1930s to emulate the Swedish experiment in the U.S. would have been laughed at. In the context of a general dislike of big government that made Orwell's *1984* a popular political fantasy, the Swedish policy goals and activities described above would have seemed like the epitome of the Big-Brother-is-watching-you scenario, and still would to many. Several of these proposed activities would have outraged many U.S. subpopulations, especially religious groups, and still would to a lesser degree. Also, there was no federal system in place at the time to implement such a far-reaching policy; today there is a large system in place, but it has a growing reputation of inefficiency that inclines many to suspect that the country is just too large to be managed efficiently centrally.

Nonetheless, the Swedish experiment was watched with envy by those who saw increasing family problems go unattended at the federal level in the U.S. It planted the notion that there could be something such as a "family" policy—a novel idea that appealed deeply to a pluralistic society that uniformly valued the family highly and that was beginning to worry about whether the family was dying or just changing. The notion that there could be a *family* policy elevated to consciousness the fact that American tradition from unwritten common law to contemporary federal legislation had focused on individuals, which by no means was intended to denigrate the family, but which did constitute an error of omission of potentially large dimensions.

EARLY AMERICAN WRITERS

The notion that there could be a family policy and the realization that we had none evoked a startle response because the family had not been neglected in professional and scientific communities. In Chapter 1 it was shown that there had been an intense, continuous interest in the family in sciences, professions, and fields of endeavor such as sociology, social welfare, and mental hygiene. Yet clearly we had no explicit family policy, and somehow it seemed that we should. European innovations were continuing and illustrations of family damage in the U.S. from nonfamily policies were beginning to surface.

The first American article on family public policy, which was to be widely quoted in subsequent years, was written by Daniel Patrick Moynihan in 1965. Fresh from his position as Assistant Secretary of Labor and en route to the U.S. Senate via the United Nations, this well-known social scientist wrote in the context of high economic stability (53 straight months of economic expansion) about the ripe opportunity for starting family social policy initiatives. He cited the traditional U.S. policy orientation to individuals and the European initiatives in family policy. He attributed the lag in U.S. policy to the difficulty of fitting policy to diverse family styles in our pluralistic society. Yet, he believed, the sound economy was being joined by an increasingly favorable political climate. He quoted liberally from a precedent-setting address by President Johnson at Howard University about the importance of, and neglect of, the American family.

Moynihan's principal example of the negative effects of having no explicit family policy was the AFDC program, which was seen as a poor alternative to European income support programs. AFDC (Aid to Families with Dependent Children—the largest component of U.S. "welfare") supported broken families *after* they had collapsed, excluding in its first 25 years families with employable males in the home. "I venture to say that in Canada—not to mention Great Britain and France—such an arrangement would be viewed as a form of social insanity."

To improve on that state of affairs, Moynihan saw initial family policy as a general statement of intent rather than a specific solution:

> A national family policy need only declare that it is the policy of the American government to promote the stability and well-being of the American family; that the social programs of the federal government will be formulated and administered with this object in mind; and finally that the President, or some person designated by him, perhaps the Secretary of Health, Education and Welfare, will report to the Congress on the condition of the American Family in all its many facets—not of *the* American family, for there is as yet no such thing, but rather of the great range of American families in terms of regions, national origins and economic status.

Under the editorship of Marvin Sussman, the entire February, 1967, issue of *Journal of Marriage and the Family* was devoted to the topic of public policy and the family. The following is a list of article titles from that issue (followed by the surnames of the authors).

"Government Policy and the Family" (Cohen and Connery)
"Mental Health and the Family" (Vincent)
"Government Health Programs Affecting the American Family" (Roemer)
"Governmental Health Programs Affecting the Family: Some New Dimensions for Governmental Action" (Morris)
"Government Economic Programs and Family Life" (Schottland)
"Education and the Family" (Shostak)
"Housing Policy and the Family" (Glazer)
"Social Authority and the Family" (Mencher)
"The Outlook for the American Family" (Pollak)

Since their publication, these articles have been quoted liberally; however, it appears that the Cohen and Connery article has been cited most frequently. Interestingly, the focus of this article is not on family problems to which federal policies can come to the rescue; instead, it focuses on the need for a healthy society for which the family is the *solution*. The following extended quotation from the summary illustrates this orientation, which was rather unique for the times (Cohen & Connery, 1967):

To compound this problem, the challenge comes at a moment in our history when traditional sources of values, such as religion, are declining in influence and when the products of scientific inquiries are daily overturning cherished beliefs.

We suspect that a revitalization of the family represents a neglected opportunity in the resolution of this crisis. As an institution it has demonstrated a remarkable resilience and a capacity to adapt to a wide range of circumstances. It has provided a transition experience for the individual that has linked past, present, and future. It has been a major source of cultural innovation and has proved its worth in the most simple and complex societies. Studies of values and attitudes have persistently demonstrated that the family is the primary source of both our individual and collective orientations and that this institution must be engaged if we are to achieve a lasting modification of values.

Yet if the family is to fulfill this need, it must be restored to a central place in our perception of the nature of our society and provided with the resources which will make possible the fulfillment of this role. This can only be accomplished by a major shift in government policy and action with respect to the family.

As the authors observe the uncertain steps being taken to translate these aspirations into reality, they are struck with the fact that, while the peoples of the world differ greatly in their class, cultural, and political orientations, they share a family life experience the similarities of which far exceed its differences. Perhaps this common bond can provide the basis not only for the regeneration of our society but also for the realization of a world community.

Alvin Schorr's 1968 book on social policy reiterated the dominance of the individual in U.S. policy and cultural diversity, as stated earlier by other authors. Additionally, he accented the dominance of another American tradition that has mitigated against the development of family-oriented public policy:

If an individualistic tradition had not tended to subordinate family goals in the national ethos, dedication to PRIVATE ENTERPRISE (written large) and government (written small) would in any case have made family goals difficult to achieve. One might regard the United States as a vast experiment in which two variables have been economic development (including industrialization and urbanization) and the structure and internal relationships of families. It is apparent that, in the United States as elsewhere, the family has been the dependent variable—stripping itself of kin, yielding one institutional function after another (economic, educational), and deepening its personality functions as the economy required a more compact and mobile unit. Though the family has also influenced the economy, the main direction of change—from economy to family—has nevertheless seemed clear. The achievement of family goals would, therefore, have required a degree of government intervention in the economy that would not have been regarded as acceptable until the comparatively recent past.

Ellen Winston, a former Commissioner of DHEW's Welfare Association, wrote in 1969 of the lack of an explicit public policy on families, citing as earlier authors had the individual tradition of public policy and European innovations. She found it particularly unfortunate that the 1960 President's Commission on National Goals had entirely missed the family. Instead of a specific problem-solving approach to family policy development, she preferred to enunciate family rights that could serve as action-guiding principles for more specific policies:

> Basic to a national policy on the family is enunciation of fundamental rights, i.e., the right of a man to a job with earnings sufficient to support his family decently; the right of a mother freely to choose whether to work or remain at home caring for her children; the right of the family, whatever its size or composition, to an adequate income, comfortable housing, privacy and independence; the same rights irrespective of geographic location or length of residence or racial background; the right to supportive community services.

As a first step, she advocated the establishment of a Commission on a National Policy on the Family, which sounds quite similar to the 1980 White House Conference on Families.

Before these family policy writers (Burns, 1956) and after them (Guillot, 1971), innumerable papers were written on the impacts of various federal programs, which qualifies them as policy analyses. Few, however, found their way into the bibliographies of the early set of family policy writers. Family policy was seen as something new, something different, something to be considered unto itself. The need for an explicit family policy had to be considered explicitly, so a new literature was born. Like so many embryonic literatures, the first offerings were heavy in philosophy and light in empirical data—groping, testing, cautious, probing. Most importantly, responses to them were favorable, thereby making it possible to escalate interest in family policy one more step.

That family policy seemed extraordinarily new is evident from the fact that few of the early writers paid any attention at all to the Social Security Act of 1935, which was and is the most significant piece of family legislation ever passed by Congress.

SENATOR MONDALE'S 1973 HEARINGS
AND CANDIDATE CARTER'S 1976 PLEDGE

On September 24, 25, and 26, 1973, Senator Walter Mondale held hearings before the Subcommittee on Children and Youth, Committee on Labor and Public Welfare, United States Senate, first session. The hearings were appropriately entitled "American Families: Trends and Pressures, 1973."

That the hearings were rooted in a concern for the welfare of children was apparent in the opening remarks of Senator Mondale:

> **Senator Mondale** The Subcommittee on Children and Youth will come to order.
>
> Today we begin 3 days of hearings on the trends and pressures affecting American families, predicated upon the simple belief that nothing is more important to a child than a healthy family.

During my 9 years in the Senate, I have probably devoted more of my time to working with the problems of children than to any other issue. I have seen many ways in which public and private programs have helped children and many other ways in which they can and should help them. But as good as some of our public and private institutions can be—and we have some excellent schools and foster homes—it has become increasingly clear to me that there is just no substitute for a healthy family—nothing else that can give a child as much love, support, confidence, motivation or feeling of self-worth and self-respect.

Fourteen experts from various disciplines had been invited to introduce prepared testimony and to engage in dialogue with members of Senator Mondale's Committee. They were:

Vincent Barabba, Director, Bureau of the Census
Andrew Billingsley, Professor of Sociology, Howard University
Harvey Brazer, Professor of Economics, Institute of Policy Studies, University of Michigan
Urie Bronfenbrenner, Professor of Human Development and Family Studies, Cornell University
Robert Coles, Psychiatrist, Harvard University
Gunnar Dybwad, Professor of Human Development, Brandeis University
Sophie Engel, Consultant, Council of Jewish Federations and Welfare Funds
William Genne, Coordinator of Family Ministries, National Council of Churches
Chris Hobgood, Pastor, First Christian Church, Alexandria, Virginia
James McHugh, Director, Family Life Division, National Conference of Catholic Charities
Margaret Mead, Curator Emeritus, American Museum of Natural History
James O'Toole, Assistant Professor of Management, University of Southern California
George Williams, Executive Director, Parents Without Partners
Edward Zigler, Department of Psychology, Yale University

To illustrate the variety of views, opinions, recommendations, and values of the participants, the following seven excerpts are offered:

Harvey Brazer I suspect that the present income tax, despite its obvious shortcomings, is not a major influence on family stability. But it does seem to be both inequitable and potentially disruptive of an institution that has served our society well, for the most part, to continue in the tax law those features that permit tax liability to turn in some appreciable measure on one's marital status.

It distresses me to think that A may never marry X on advice of their tax accountant.

Senator Mondale Is it your thesis that divorce is good business under the present tax laws then?

Mr. Brazer My wife and I have been calculating, Mr. Chairman, and clearly we would change nothing except the legal nature of our relationship. In the case of our circumstances, we would save enough per year to meet the cost of sending one of our children through college. What I am talking about is a tax saving of about $2,000 and $3,000 a year.

Urie Bronfenbrenner Among families that are intact and well-off economically, and, of course, predominantly white, research results indicate that parents are spending less time in activity with their children.

For example, a survey of changes in childrearing practices in the United States over a 25-year period reveals a decrease in all spheres of interaction between parent and child. A similar trend is indicated by data from cross-cultural studies comparing American families with their European counterparts. Thus in a comparative study of socialization practices among German and American parents, the former emerged as significantly more involved in activities with their children, including both affection and discipline. A second study, conducted several years later, showed changes over time in both cultures reflecting "a trend toward the dissolution of the family as a social system," with Germany moving closer to the American pattern of "centrifugal forces pulling the members into relationships outside the family."

The forces undermining the parental role are particularly strong in the case of fathers. For example, although in one interview study of middle class families, fathers reported spending an average of 15 to 20 minutes a day playing with their one year old infants, an observational research revealed a rather different story: the data indicate that fathers spend relatively little time interacting with their infants. The mean number of interactions per day was 2.7, and the average number of seconds per day was 37.7.

Robert Coles It seems to me that with regard to welfare families, we all know that in many states and communities it serves the interest of a poor family and a jobless family for the mother to be separated from the father so that she can have a degree of support. But my experience with those families has been that this is not a premeditated thing; that the economic stress upon the family comes first, that the families then collapse under the weight of that, the joblessness, the idleness, the loss of self-respect that Professor O'Toole documented so well. Then when the family is fragmented and torn asunder, the welfare law comes in and the family gets support and this separation is given new sanction and support and a kind of secondary gain.

James McHugh . . . government policy should respect the pluralism of family heritages and family styles. Otto Pollak maintains that the function that has truly been taken away from families is the autonomy of setting its own standards. The family has been subjected to the tinkering of the social experimenters, the ineptitude of the bureaucrats and domination by self-proclaimed specialists.

It is time for the family to assert its own power against the expert, and protect itself against becoming simply one more factor in the utopian schemes of today's social planners.

Margaret Mead If you look at the budget or look at an analysis of what we are doing, you will find the family does not appear anywhere. We have child care, health, food, housing, in separate categories, but no place even where children are properly gathered together any more, and no place at all for the family.

I remember going in 1944 to a home economic exhibit of beautiful white kitchens, sanitary, well designed, and I looked the kitchen over and I said, "But where do you put the baby?'' There was no place to hang it up or sit it down, and in some cases it might have gotten lost under the icebox.

I asked all those professionals why there was no place for the baby in that newly designed American kitchen, and they said, "Because there is no Bureau of Family Life in the U.S. Department of Agriculture."

This was in 1944 and we are still in the same position. There is no focus that looks after the family as a whole, although there are many programs that look at particular problems, the disadvantaged children or disadvantaged old people, but they are specialized programs and nobody brings them together.

I think that what we are now ready to do what I assume this whole investigation is about, to make the family a focal point and ask what every other type of legislation is doing to the family.

James O'Toole In summary, the evidence is overwhelming that unemployment and underemployment among breadwinners is the primary factor leading to continued marital instability among the poor. The absence of work or work that fails to fulfill the function of economic security, self-esteem, identity, and a sense of mastery over the chaos of one's environment, will not provide the stable basis required to build a lasting familial relationship.

Edward Zigler I agree with many others who feel that a variety of historical, economic, and social factors as well as current pressures make family life in America more difficult today than it once was. I refer here to the decline of the extended family, to the extremely important phenomenon of the ever-increasing number of working mothers, to the increased mobility which has come to characterize the American people, and to those types of urbanization and suburbanization that tend to isolate American families one from another. All of these phenomena have taken away supports that families once relied upon. The wisdom of grandparents, aunts, and uncles is no longer readily available to young families. The children of working mothers are without an essential nurturant figure for many hours of the day. The life of a mobile family is burdened with discontinuity and upheaval. Our communities are likewise in a state of flux, so that families once able to rely on the immediate neighborhood for assistance in childrearing or crisis intervention find that they are no longer able to do so.

These excerpts, of course, are a very small sampler of all the testimony introduced by all the participants. Yet the pieces are there for a four-point scenario that seems to describe the total testimony.

1. Family problems are enormous. Financial stability is constantly threatened by unemployment and underemployment; the quality of parenting, measured simply by time spent with children, is believed to have declined; life-supporting and life-directing ideals have been badly tarnished; and so on.
2. Natural support systems have been weakened.
3. Government support systems have not explicitly addressed family life in their policies. Some government programs hurt some families, such as *ex post facto* "welfare" programs that sanction the dissolved family and tax structures that tempt the bold middle-class family with savvy to cope with college expenses to consider divorce.

4. A massive societal rebuilding job is ahead of us that must balance family-sensitive government policies with protection of family self-determination.

It would be difficult to underestimate the importance of these hearings. They carried the family policy idea from rhetoric in occasional political speeches to the dignified status of formal consideration before a significant committee of the U.S. Senate. They provided visibility to a select few family experts; they encouraged many others to begin serious investments of time and expertise in this new and promising field. Also, both the fact of the hearings and the influence of their sponsors undoubtedly inclined Candidate Carter to promise in the 1976 campaign a White House Conference on Families.

Carter's Manchester, New Hampshire, speech on the family during the 1976 campaign evoked such widespread interest that Joseph Califano, a future Secretary of HEW, was directed to compile a report on the status of the American family. Interestingly, unemployment, which had risen during the Nixon-Ford administration, was fingered in Califano's report (September 17, 1976) as the principal problem plaguing American families and it was the rise in unemployment four years later that became a central issue in the 1980 campaign.

EXPLOSION OF PROFESSIONAL INTEREST

The stimulation provided by the early writers and the sanctions provided by the Mondale hearings led to a massive increase in the attention to family policy in the professional literature. A very small sampling of this outpouring of the international literature, family impact analysis, and U.S. journals and books is considered here.

The International Literature

As pioneering efforts in other countries increased, so did the interest among American professionals and scientists. Indeed, some unusual interactions developed. Moroney, a North Carolina social scientist, was commissioned by an English group to examine the question of family dependency on the state, specifically: "Is the family today less willing or less able to care for its severely dependent members, for instance frail old people or mentally handicapped children?" From the summary of his intriguing book (1976):

> In summary, there is no evidence that the family as such is giving up its caring function. There has been and continues to be more inter- and intra-generational contact and support than many believe to exist, despite the fact that families are required to be mobile; that fewer caretakers are available because of higher marriage rates and working mothers; that families wanting to care for elderly parents find this difficult if not impossible because of long-standing housing policies; and finally that community social services tend to be provided to indi-

viduals who either have no family or whose family has reached a decision to discontinue the caring function. The family appears to be stronger and more viable than many anticipated. This in turn has led others to suggest that the State is exploiting the family. Exploitation is, however, a strong word. It implies that the State consciously and purposely sets out to use the family unjustly for its own profit or advantage, that the State is benefiting at the expense of the family. There is no doubt that the state is benefiting. The amount of social care provided by families far exceeds that undertaken by the State. It is impossible, furthermore, to assign a monetary value to it, and it is inconceivable to speculate the cost involved if the State were to become the primary caring institution. Furthermore, the State through its social welfare system cannot take over one of the most basic social functions, the provision of emotional support. Some family functions can be substituted for—for example physical care, whether this involves the provision of meals, housekeeping, a residence, recreation and income maintenance. The State is also in the position to support the family, to relieve the burden of the caring function by substituting for certain functions. Earlier the case was made that a caring society must involve some sense of a shared responsibility. The essence of sharing is a recognition of the contribution that families are making and a serious attempt to move from a unilateral relationship to one based on exchange. The State is fortunate to have families who care. The corollary to this is that families should also be supported by a caring society.

This view of the interdependence of the family and the state is midway between the extremes of those who favor the powerful, benevolent state that will care for its ailing members and those who look at the state from the family's viewpoint of control or selective consumption.

In the most ambitious effort to date, Kamerman and Kahn (1978) compiled articles on the state of family policy in 14 countries, ranked in three sets by degree of explicitness of policy. This is a good introduction to family policy because it quickly disabuses the neophyte of rosy expectations. In spite of getting there first, other countries have yet to develop an ideal model for late starters to emulate. Indeed, it is the opinion here that no country has yet developed a "good" family policy model. It is something of a letdown to find the same issues in countries with family policies as in countries without—poverty, children's rights, disability, care of the elderly, day care, tax inequities, housing, adolescent turmoil, and, in general, the best division of labor between the family and the state for managing problems. Probably the most important conclusion to be drawn from Kamerman and Kahn's book is that the road to family policy is not an easy one, and it is probable that the principal reasons for working toward one are that not doing so is intolerable and that the importance of the goal justifies the agonizing first steps.

Family Impact Analysis

No systematic attempt to work toward national family policies can ignore the need for an on-going analysis of the planned and actual impact of implemented federal policies on the family. One approach, advocated by

Kamerman (1976), would be the development of a "family impact statement" for all relevant federal legislation, modeled somewhat after the current environmental impact statement for the protection of the natural environment. According to Kamerman:

> *Formulation*—A family impact statement would involve analysis of selected pending legislation, policies, regulations, programs, in order to make explicit:
>   —the potential effects or outcomes, both negative and positive, (with stress on the negative) of actions taken or pending (laws, policies, regulations) that might impinge on families (directly or indirectly);
>   —the potential for unanticipated consequences (both negative and positive) of such actions; and
>   —the potential lack of coherence or conflict with existing laws, policies, and programs.
> *Summary*—All governmental activity, in some way, takes account of consequences or impacts. The form may be descriptive, rhetorical, financial, or other. The family impact statement is intended to improve this process.
> Development of a family impact statement is predicated on the assumption that it would be worthwhile to try to predict the likely consequences of government activity for families, and that the process of prediction could be improved over time. Successful development of a family impact statement requires a systematic policy analysis in which consequences are made explicit. Alternative values would be identified, with an indication of how each could be realized or what the consequences of potential actions might be for varying sets of values. Where choices conflict, the final decision would have to be made in the political arena.
> The ultimate goal of a family impact statement should be to improve the conditions of families. The method selected to achieve this is to influence decision-making regarding public policy for families and children. Thus, the immediate goal of a family impact statement should be to raise national consciousness regarding policies affecting families and children by making the consequences of public policies explicit.

A continuous effort at family impact analysis has been underway at the George Washington University's Family Impact Seminar, directed by A. Sidney Johnson, III—the principal staffer for Senator Mondale's hearings. An early endeavor by Johnson's group attempted to create an inventory of federal programs that have an impact on families (Johnson et al., 1978). Their initial source of information was the catalogue of Federal Domestic Assistance, which described 1044 federal programs. Only two programs were found under "Family" in the subject index: family medicine and family planning. Further investigation, however, revealed 268 programs that "'provided financial assistance, in-kind subsidies, or varied services directed to individuals or families who were thus the intended beneficiaries.'" These programs were housed in 17 federal departments or agencies, HEW being the leader (119 programs) and VA (31), Housing and Urban Development (24), Labor (21), and Agriculture (19) in second through fifth places. Sixty-three of the 268 programs were judged to have "explicit" family policies—the nature and the degree of explicitness were not stated.

It is interesting that Johnson et al. found it desirable to catalogue the 268 programs according to which of three family impact dimensions were involved:

> *Membership Dimension.* In this column we considered whether the program had the potential to have an effect on families' membership trends (birth, marriage, separation, divorce, death) or household composition (which family members live together). Examples of programs with impact on this dimension would be family planning, abortion, health services, foster care, child abuse and neglect programs, community-based services for mental health or the penal system.

> *Material Support Functions Dimension.* In this column we checked those programs which affect families' abilities to provide material support for their members through employment, securing of housing, job training. These include, for example, income maintenance programs, housing subsidies, and job training programs.

> *Nurturant Health Functions Dimension.* A third dimension of impact clusters around the function of families to rear and nurture their dependents, encourage and support their physical, intellectual and emotional development and provide psychological sustenance to their members. Programs which exemplify the various kinds of impact on such functions are nutrition and preventive health programs; compensatory education and programs providing services to vulnerable family members such as the handicapped, mentally ill, elderly, young children.

Johnson et al. are quite convincing about the fact that the U.S., by having many family-relevant programs, has not totally neglected the family in its policies. Yet, an inspection of the programs that are reported as having an "explicit" family policy suggests here a rather mild degree of explicitness. This, in turn, raises the question of whether explicitness is a dichotomous variable without gradations (something either is explicit or it isn't) or whether it is a continuous variable with infinite shades of explicitness—an issue virtually ignored in the literature.

Journals

Professional journal articles on family policy issues became so numerous after Mondale's hearings as to be almost uncountable. Several journals, in an attempt to be comprehensive, devoted entire issues to the subject, including the *Journal of Marriage and the Family* in 1979 (to update its 1967 issue cited above). The lists of articles in three such journals are provided here to illustrate what the editors considered to be a comprehensive set of articles.

Daedalus (Journal of the American Academy of Arts and Sciences)—Spring, 1977:
  "A Biosocial Perspective on Parenting" (Rossi)
  "The Child in the Family" (Kagan)
  "Family Time and Historical Time" (Hareven)
  "Reflections on the History of the Family" (Wrigley)

"Ghosts, Kin, and Progeny: Some Features of Family Life in Early Modern France" (Davis)

"Economic Perspectives on the Family" (Sawhill)

"Pied Piper Politics and the Child-Care Debate" (Woolsey)

"Income Support Policies and the Family" (Blaydon and Stack)

"The Impact of Housing Policies on Family Life in the United States since World War II" (Downs)

"Some Aspects of the Contemporary Japanese Family: Once Confucian, Now Fatherless?" (Wagatsuma)

"Changing Life Styles in Kenya" (Whiting)

"The Family and the City" (Aries)

Journal of Marriage and the Family—August, 1979 (a partial list):

"Should the United States Have an Explicit Family Policy? A Symposium"

"Why We Need a Family Policy" (Feldman)

"What Price National Policy for Families" (Leik and Hill)

"The Issue of Family Policy: Do We Know Enough to Take Action?" (Moroney)

"Views of Family Policy" (Schorr)

"Implementation of a National Family Policy: The Role of the Social Scientist" (Tallman)

"Family Policy Research: Emergent Models and Some Theoretical Issues" (Nye and McDonald)

"Policy, Social Policy, and Family Policy: Concepts, Concerns and Analytic Tools" (Zimmerman)

"European and United States Political Contexts for Family Policy Research" (Dumon and Aldous)

"Legislators' Attitudes Toward Family Policy" (Zimmerman, Mattessich, and Leik)

"Public Assistance, Female Headship, and Economic Well-Being" (Bradbury et al.)

"The Effects of Welfare on Marital Stability and Remarriage" (Bahr)

"Family Impacts of the 1975 Recession: Duration of Unemployment" (Moen)

"The Impact of the Legal System on Adjustment to Marital Separation" (Spanier and Anderson)

"The Family-Oriented Policy and Treatment Program for Female Juvenile Status Offenders" (Druckman)

"The Family and Federal Drug Abuse Policies-Programs: Toward Making the Invisible Family Visible" (Clayton)

"Day Care in the Next Decade: 1980-1990" (Hofferth)

Social Work—November, 1979:
  "An Initial Agenda for Family Policy" (Gilbert)
  "Perspectives on Family Policy"
    "Complexities of Family Policy: What Can Be Done" (Padberg)
    "The Case Against Family Policy" (Barbaro)
  "Family Structure"
    "Female-Headed Families: Trends and Implications" (Wattenberg and
      Reinhardt)
    "Children and Divorce: A Review" (Wallerstein and Kelly)
  "Family Planning"
    "Bioethical Issues in Family Planning" (Brieland)
    "Abortion Work: Strains, Coping Strategies, Policy Implications"
      (Joffe)
    "Teenage Pregnancy: A Research Review" (Chilman)
  "Child Care and Protection"
    "Defining the Care in Child Care" (Authier)
    "Comparative Analysis in Family Policy: A Case Study" (Kamerman
      and Kahn)
    "Effective Treatment of Child Abuse and Neglect" (Cohn)
  "Care and Support for the Elderly and Handicapped"
    "Community Care and Deinstitutionalization: A Review" (Segal)
    "Deinstitutionalization: Those Left Behind" (Morell)
    "Family Supports in Old Age" (Monk)
  "Income Maintenance"
    "The Family Life Cycle and Economic Security" (Axinn and Levin)
    "Welfare Policies and Black Families" (Trader)
  "Research Parameters"
    "Typology for Family Policy Research" (McDonald)

Unlike the early literature, which dealt globally with the need for a
family policy, the literature in these three journals has begun to get down to
specifics. Collectively, 20 different topics were approached. Only three topics
received major attention in four or more articles—the need for and appropriateness of family policy, economic dimensions of family life, and international perspectives. Many topics of enormous importance unto themselves
(e.g., housing, drug abuse, and aging) received only one article apiece. The
literature in these three journals reflects general maturation. It collectively
demonstrates the enormous scope of topics that must be considered as part of
family policy and they demonstrate how far we are from in-depth analysis of
any one topic.

Perhaps the most interesting reflection of the maturation of the literature
is the divided opinion on the appropriateness and feasibility of developing a

comprehensive family policy. The early writers had focused on the absence of a family policy in this country, the precedents for one in other countries, and the gut feeling that maybe we should do something about the situation. The articles by Feldman and Moroney, however, point to the difficulty of formulating one policy that will fit the various forms of the contemporary American family and, indeed, to the "variant" forms of families that used to be called "deviant," which must be explicitly included or excluded from the definition of family—a controversial issue, to say the least. Barbaro assumes the role of devil's advocate and argues against a comprehensive family policy. He also alludes to the pluralism of family life-styles, to which no single policy can be fit, and argues that the nature of our political system makes possible only a watered-down policy for potentially sensitive topics such as the "family."

A review of the titles of these articles yields a conclusion similar to the one above for Kamerman and Kahn's book on 14 countries. The topics are the same old topics: housing, poverty, disability, childrearing, divorce. It appears that, when one gets down to specifics, the traditionally important issues dominate because the family dimension is just one dimension of each issue. Perhaps the value of family public policy lies in making the family dimension of public issues so explicit that issue-specific policies not only avoid inadvertently hurting the family but also purposefully strengthen it. Family public policy additionally enables one to cluster public issues by degree of relevance to the family—a feasible exercise of probable great significance. But whether the family by itself constitutes a public issue deserving a public policy is still open to debate.

Books

Many of the references above were to book-length treatises and they collectively seem to mirror the topics and concerns of the articles, and reinforce the same conclusions. Kanter (1977), for instance, wrote an insightful review of the issue of work and the family, wherein she provided some historical and theoretical perspectives and discussed the reciprocal influences that work and the family have on each other. A principal component of her concluding chapter is a listing of areas needing "policy" experiments, which included:

Flexible working hours
Organizational change and job redesign
Joint family and work-group meetings and workshops
Bringing children (and spouses) to work
On-work-site counseling
Community supports for employed children
Leaves and sabbaticals
Workmen's compensation for families of work "victims"
"Family responsibility statements" by organizations

When one gets down to the specific issue of work and social welfare, there is a family dimension that is often overlooked. Consequently, Kanter recommends policy experiments to improve the fate of families with working members, which would also benefit the workplace. She does not concern herself with the larger topic of the need for a comprehensive, explicit family policy, but rather with the family dimension of the issue of work and social welfare. The quality and specificity of her work reinforce the conclusion above that advances in family policy will probably proceed issue by issue. Whether the accumulation of these individual endeavors will ever yield a comprehensive family policy that is more than innocuously platitudinous depends on one's opinion on whether the whole is more than the sum of its parts and whether that whole can be appropriately and effectively approached by our present political system. No consensus on that has emerged in the professional/scientific literature.

At the same time, no simple dichotomy of public policy into "comprehensive" and "specific issue" will long endure. Policies regarding such issues as disability, housing, and income maintenance overlap, making clusterings at higher levels desirable. Policies for each issue can be broken down into program-specific policies—e.g., each disability program has a policy of its own and ideally should be compatible with other program-specific disability policies, all of which should ideally be subsumed within an overall disability policy. How much "layering" and "cross-integrating" of policies is possible and desirable is a topic largely unexplored in the contemporary literature.

DISCUSSION AND SUMMARY

Logically one may ask what the prevailing thought is on whether we have an explicit family policy, whether we should have one, whether it is feasible to create one, and what form it should take. Clearly there is consensus that the United States does not have, and never has had, an explicit, comprehensive family policy, yet this seems somewhat overdone. The U.S. is still very new at formal policy setting and there are few contemporary issues for which we have a clear, formal, explicit, comprehensive policy. Additionally, many federal programs reflecting policies of all shades of explicitness have family implications that are so obvious that some feel that they need little explication—e.g., Workmen's Compensation (for injury on the job) and unemployment insurance. Do we have an explicit, comprehensive family policy? No, but perhaps that isn't so surprising.

There are many schools of thought about the desirability of creating an explicit family policy. On the favorable side are those who simply find the notion that we don't have one unacceptable, those who want to catch up to the Europeans, those who are concerned that the lack of explicit attention tends to produce programs that under-consider the family or inadvertently hurt it, and those who want family issues—*qua* family issues—to receive formal policy consideration. On the negative side are those who consider the family sacrosanct and of no concern to meddling, big government. In the neutral position are those who find all this talk about policy distracting and pedantic— they just want government to recognize family problems and to react responsively; therefore, they are more positive than negative. Although there is no consensus, there appears to be a sizable majority who want government to at least move in the direction of more explicit policy, as long as that means a more systematic, more responsible approach by government to family problems.

There is no consensus on how feasible an explicit family policy is. Regarding one overall family policy, there are those who favor a simple declaration of favorable intent (e.g., Moynihan above) and those who reject a single, global policy as simultaneously ill-suited for pluralistic American family life-styles and the multitude of individually legislated federal programs. Regarding individually developed "fractional" policies for specific issues, most seem to favor them as a way of moving sensibly and safely toward explicitness of policy—e.g., reforming the tax structure to remove the "marriage penalty." Indeed, there are those, such as Johnson et al. (1978), who believe we already have such "fractional" policies in hundreds of federal programs.

There is no consensus on what form a policy should take. Regarding a single overall policy, there are those who prefer, again, a simple statement of favorable intent. There are precedents for the adoption of something like a Family Bill of Rights or a Family Charter, such as the Family Service Association of America proposed decades ago ("The Family Is Basic . . . ," 1961). Something a little short of a single, global family policy might be an omnibus family act (one such act has been introduced into Congress by Senator Laxalt and is discussed in Chapter 4). Regarding a set of fractional policies, there are those who favor dealing with family issues one at a time, formulating a specific, evaluatable policy for each issue in each piece of legislation. Perhaps most favor some combination of these forms. A simple, global statement of intent never hurts and sanctions the whole idea, and a "bill of rights" could be formulated in such a way as to provide general action-guiding principles. Sooner or later, however, one has to get down to specific issues with specific statements of the problem and specific goals if family impact is to be carefully analyzed. Lack of consensus here reflects lack of consensus in the larger policy community about what a policy is, what alternative forms it can take, and what the strengths and weaknesses are for each alternative form.

The trends in all of this are quite clear. The federal government has increasingly assumed a large role for protecting the health and well-being of the U.S. population; "policy analysis" has become the popular term applied to understanding how this role is played and how well. In the absence of a formal family cog in the policy machinery, various errors of omission and commission are being identified. Both political and scientific/professional communities have passed the water-testing stage. The precipitant for the escalating interest in family policy was to be the 1980 White House Conference on Families. Before considering this monumental historical event, however, some family policy issues deserve to be considered to isolate some of the critical dimensions of family public policy.

Chapter 3

The Dimensions of Public Policy: Some Issues

Since we are primarily interested in chronicling the emergence of family public policy, detailed analyses of contemporary policy issues are not provided in these chapters. Indeed, a thorough analysis of any single issue such as housing or divorce deserves its own book-length treatise. Yet, an appreciation of the dimensions of public policy requires at least some consideration of individual issues, so this chapter is devoted to a small, somewhat random selection of profiles of family-relevant policy issues.

Moderate detail is provided on the issue of abortions. Somewhat less detail is provided on the issues of disability and poverty. Short, undetailed profiles are offered on several other issues. The discussion at the end of the chapter abstracts from these profiles to some of the major dimensions of family public policy.

ABORTIONS AND UNWANTED PREGNANCIES

Few issues over the past decade have divided the country as sharply as the abortion issue. On the one side are the "anti" forces, principally religious groups such as the "pro-life" movement; on the other side are the "pro-choice" forces, an unorganized assemblage of feminist groups, professional groups, and would-be consumers. The battles between them have been waged mainly in the courts, and the principal contested issues have been 1) whether abortion should be allowed at all, 2) whether public funds should be used for abortions, 3) whether adolescents should have access to abortion without parental consent, and 4) whether there is equal access among all subpopulations to abortion providers.

The Issue of the Legality of Abortions

Prior to 1970, abortions were virtually illegal throughout the country, with just a few states offering a few exceptions, mainly for therapeutic, life-saving abortions. From 1970 to 1973, numerous successful challenges to conservative state laws gradually expanded the availability of legal abortions. A landmark decision occurred on January 22, 1973, when the Supreme Court ruled in *Roe* v. *Wade* and *Doe* v. *Bolton* that the restrictive Texas and Georgia abortions laws were unconstitutional, thereby nullifying all restrictive abortion laws. From that time to this, the legality of abortions has not been challenged successfully in the courts.

Consumption of abortion services has increased with their court-ordered availability, as the following demonstrates (*Abortion Surveillance,* 1980):

	No. Abortions	No. Abortions per 1000 live births
1969	22,670	6.3
1970	193,491	51.9
1971	485,816	136.6
1972	586,760	180.1
1973	615,831	196.3
1974	763,476	241.6
1975	854,853	271.9
1976	988,267	312.0
1977	1,079,430	324.5
1978	1,157,776	347.0

The growth in consumer demand for abortions has been large and continuous. At present there is roughly one abortion for every three live births.

[A note about the data. There are two principal information systems that annually update national abortion statistics. One is in the Center for Disease Control (CDC) in Atlanta, which is part of the U.S. Public Health Service. The other is in the Alan Guttmacher Institute (AGI) in New York—a private organization. The CDC gets its information from state agencies, whereas AGI obtains reports directly from providers and does the more complete job of enumerating abortions annually; CDC's estimates are usually about 85% of AGI's, so that the data above slightly underenumerate U.S. abortions. The total number of abortions annually is generally estimated now at 1.5 million.]

This magnitude of abortion consumption places the U.S. in an intermediate position relative to developed countries. Forrest, Sullivan, and Tietze (1979a,b) listed abortion rates for selected countries several years ago (the abortion rate is the number of abortions per 1000 women of ages 15–44 in a year).

7.8	Scotland
10.6	Canada
10.6	England and Wales

16.7	Finland
16.8	Tunisia
19.3	Sweden
19.7	Norway
22.0	East Germany
24.3	Denmark
26.9	*United States*
28.0	Czechoslovakia
28.4	Singapore
39.2	Hungary
61.0	Cuba
64.5	Bulgaria

Some of the characteristics of abortion consumers are provided below from both AGI and CDC data (*Abortion Surveillance*, 1979; Forrest et al., 1979a,b; *Abortion Surveillance*, 1980):

	AGI	CDC
No. of abortions	1,409,600	1,157,776
Abortion rate (no. of abortions per 1000 females ages 15–44)	27	22
Abortion ratio (abortions per 1000 live births)	400	324.5
No. of providers:	2716	
Metro	2156	
Non-metro	560	
By % of age:		100.0
Under 15		1.2
15–19		29.3
20–24		34.1
25–29		18.5
30–34		9.4
35–39		4.7
Over 39		1.7
Unknown		1.0
% by race:		100.0
White		63.5
Black and other		32.2
Unknown		4.3
% marital status:		100.0
Married		23.7
Unmarried		73.9
Unknown		2.4

The Issue of Government Support of Abortions

On the assumption that medically indigent women deserve equal access to legal medical services, Medicaid–Title XIX of the Social Security Act, which

Table 2. Estimated number of abortions and total expenditures under Medicaid, by state, FY 1977[a]

State	No. of abortions	Expenditures
Total	294,600	$86,776,400
Ala.	1,000	174,300
Alaska*	300*	17,600*
Ariz.	†	†
Ark.	600	94,700‡
Calif.	101,000‡	40,100,000‡
Colo.	2,800*	333,200
Conn.	1,700	407,600
Del.	700‡	250,000‡
D.C.	5,600	1,547,900
Fla.	4,500	652,200
Ga.	6,600	712,500
Hawaii	1,500	242,400
Idaho	100	25,800
Ill.	21,400	3,148,200
Ind.	u	u
Iowa	900	300,000
Kans.	3,000	721,100
Ky.	1,900	418,400
La.	0	0
Maine	400	45,000
Md.	6,000	1,300,000
Mass.	4,400	667,500
Mich.	15,000	3,105,300
Minn.	1,900	480,500
Miss.	u	u
Mo.	2,500‡	181,400‡
Mont.	500	102,000

(continued)

is the principal source of federal funds for health care in the Department of Health and Human Services (HHS), began paying for abortions in nearly all states. By fiscal year (FY) 1977, this had increased to 294,600 Medicaid-supported abortions. (See Table 2 for a state breakdown of 1977 Medicaid-supported abortions.)

Table 2 (*Continued*)

State	No. of abortions	Expenditures
Nebr.	500	129,000
Nev.	400	156,800
N.H.	200	45,600
N.J.	11,000	4,100,000
N. Mex.	500	86,900
N.Y.	50,000‡	17,200,000
N.C.	1,500	991,100
N. Dak.	u	u
Ohio	10,000*	2,000,000
Okla.	700*	93,000
Oreg.	2,400	865,500
Pa.	13,600	2,623,100
R.I.	700	166,000
S.C.	1,000	169,800
S. Dak.	u	u
Tenn.	1,200*	274,700
Tex.	3,500	652,100
Utah	200	38,100
Vt.	300	75,000
Va.	4,000	483,200
Wash.	4,300	1,000,000
W. Va.	500	148,700
Wis.	3,700	423,700
Wyo.	100	26,500

*FY 1976.   †No Medicaid program.   ‡CY 1976.   u = Unavailable.

aReprinted by permission from: *Abortions and the Poor: Private Morality, Public Responsibility.* The Alan Guttmacher Institute, New York, 1979.

In 1977, the unchecked growth of government spending for abortions received three reversals in the executive, legislative, and judicial branches of the federal government. On June 20, 1977, the Supreme Court ruled that states and localities need not pay for nontherapeutic abortions for pregnant women, even though they pay for childbirth and other pregnancy-related expenses. On July 12, 1977, President Carter supported the Supreme Court decision and opposed government financing of abortions "except when the woman's life is threatened or when pregnancy is the result of rape or incest.'' On August 14, 1977, a federal court lifted a restraining order that had prevented enforcement of the 1976 Hyde amendment (Rep. Henry J. Hyde, R.-Ill.), which prohibited use of HEW funds to pay for abortions except to save a pregnant woman's life. A version of the Hyde amendment was attached to the 1978 Labor-HEW Appropriations bill, and was renewed in 1979. The cumulative effect of these actions was to cut federal funding for abortions to a minimum.

Interestingly, this retrenchment in public policy did not have a profound effect on the magnitude of abortion consumption. Part of this is attributable to the fact that some of the costs of the abortion service package, such as pregnancy testing, were still reimbursable under Medicaid. This reduced the price to a level affordable by many low-income women and their families. Abortions did tend to be performed slightly later in pregnancy, possibly reflecting the time needed by those women and their families to accumulate the necessary funds. Finally, Gold and Cates (1979) stated that, by February of 1979, 16 states and the District of Columbia were using their own funds for abortion, and 85% of Medicaid-eligible women lived in those states. Of course, abortion consumption among nonpoor women had also continued to rise.

The pendulum swung again on February 19, 1980, when the Supreme Court broadly and temporarily reinstated government funding for abortions under the Medicaid program. Specifically, the Supreme Court lifted a stay against a January 15, 1980, decision by District Judge John Dooling of New York that the Hyde Amendment was unconstitutional, requiring the federal government to restore federal Medicaid funding within 30 days—the final decision to be given later in the year. Medicaid funding was restored.

The final decision came on June 30, 1980, surprisingly reversing the February 19 ruling. By a 5 to 4 vote, the Court ruled that it was not unconstitutional for the U.S. Congress, through the Hyde Amendment, to exclude abortion funds from the Medicaid package, and Medicaid funds were again cut off except for life-threatening circumstances and for promptly reported pregnancies resulting from rape or incest. This ruling left standing the 1973 ruling that a woman was free to seek a legal abortion, but it made federal funding of that abortion discretionary. Thus the restrictive Hyde Amendment was constitutional, but so also would be any later change in Congress to assume financial responsibility for abortions through Medicaid or other programs.

At the time of this ruling, 10 jurisdictions were providing Medicaid-funded abortions under favorable state laws and with state funding—the District of Columbia, Maryland, North Carolina, New York, Alaska, Colorado, Hawaii, Michigan, Oregon, and Washington state. Presumably abortions for poor women would be continued in those states. In an additional 15 states—

California, most notably, in terms of numbers of abortions—state laws were still restrictive, but abortions with state funds were being provided under court order. Presumably the 1980 ruling would allow litigation to return those state laws to restrictive status.

By making government funding of abortions for poor women legislatively discretionary rather than constitutionally mandatory, the Supreme Court passed policymaking to the political community. The three 1980 presidential candidates had already declared their stances on public funds for abortions—Reagan and Carter against, Anderson for. But the greatest pressure was placed squarely on the undeclared members of Congress and state legislatures, who realized that their constituents were split on the issue and that their voting records in the years ahead might determine their political futures.

Litigation will also continue into the foreseeable future. Immediately following the June 30, 1980, ruling, advocacy groups on both sides of the issue declared their intentions of doing so. The pro-life forces promised to extend their efforts to press for a constitutional amendment that would nullify the 1973 ruling making most abortions legal, as Reagan had declared himself for but Carter had not, and to press for changes in state laws in liberal states.

The pro-choice groups would seek new grounds for challenging the constitutionality of the Hyde Amendment; the June 30, 1980, Supreme Court ruling had specifically left open the issue of constitutionally mandated government funding of abortions for poor women who sought abortions on religious grounds. These groups also would press for liberalization of state laws throughout the country. As one newspaper reporter put it, there is a war on between rival ideologies and the end is not in sight.

The Issue of Adolescents and Parental Consent

All of the legal, moral, and social issues surrounding the general topic of abortions apply equally to adolescence and are intensified by the legal issue of children's rights versus parents' rights. The right to privacy is a constitutionally protected right and has been cited in many cases about adolescents' rights to secure medical care on their own. In recent years this right to privacy had been cited in cases challenging state laws that limited the adolescent's right to secure an abortion without parental consent; e.g., *Planned Parenthood of Central Missouri* v. *Danforth,* 428 U.S. 52 (1976).

In a 1979 landmark decision, *Bellotti* v. *Baird,* the U.S. Supreme Court ruled unconstitutional by a vote of 8-1 a Massachusetts statute that provided in part:

> If the mother is less than eighteen years of age and has not married, the consent of both the mother and her parents (for an abortion) is required. If one or both of the mother's parents refuse such consent, it may be obtained by order of a judge of the superior court for good cause shown after hearing as he deems necessary.

The eight justices, however, split four and four on an alternative consent procedure. Justice Lewis F. Powell—joined by Justices Burger, Stewart, and Rehnquist—delivered the lead opinion, which proposed a consent procedure whereby an adolescent could go directly to a court or administrative agency that would decide whether she was mature enough to consent to an abortion by herself. Justice John Paul Stevens—joined by Justices Marshall, Brennan, and Blackmun—concurred that the Massachusetts statute was unconstitutional and further felt that "need to commence judicial proceedings (as outlined by Justice Stevens in the lead opinion) in order to obtain a legal abortion would impose a burden at least as great as, and probably greater than, that imposed on the minor child by the need to obtain the consent of a parent." All of which means that the courts are more agreed on what is unconstitutional than on what consent procedure, if any, *is* constitutional, which makes continued ligation into the future probable.

Not all states have brought their laws into compliance with recent Supreme Court decisions and many of those that have done so have variations on child's consent, notification of parents, and various stipulations. Scientific Analysis Corporation (*The Legal Status of Adolescents,* 1980) reviewed state laws on minors' consent to abortion and provided state-by-state capsule descriptions, which are included in the appendix at the end of this chapter.

It is not difficult to construe this court-decreed trend as the antithesis of family policy. By accenting the adolescent's rights to consume abortion services without parental notification and consent, one emphasizes the nonfamily dimension of problem solving and raises the issue of whether what an adolescent *can* do legally is the *best* form of problem solving. Especially with the very young pregnant adolescent, one wonders whether the overzealous court or agency professional who "sides" with her will inadvertently create a dependency in her on the rules of the state as a way around the customs of the family.

Theodora Ooms at the Family Impact Seminar was one of the first professional writers to assess this court-decreed trend critically. The following is taken from her forthcoming book, *Teenage Pregnancy in a Family Context: Implications for Policy* (in press):

> With regard to a minor's pregnancy, professional opinion is virtually unanimous in regarding requirement of parental notification to be a harmful and unnecessary barrier to an adolescent's obtaining treatment and a breach of her constitutional right to privacy. . . . I argue here that such a position undermines family roles and functioning. It ignores the legitimate rights of parents to attempt to help their school-age daughter at a crisis point in her life and may result in her making a decision based on incomplete information. It also makes an absolute and artificial distinction between parental responsibilities in the area of sexual behavior and all other areas of a minor child's life.
>
> Those opposed to requiring notification think that a doctor or social worker is the best person to help the teenager make this decision about her pregnancy and

whether to tell her parents. But it is her family (members) who are the most reliable sources of information about what their reaction is to the pregnancy and about what willingness and resources they have to offer to help with the baby if she should choose to have it. Her family is also more likely to be able to comment on the teenager's competence to undertake parenting responsibilities, and on the effects parenting will have on her. These are essential facts that need to be known if the teenager's decision is to be based on informed consent.

The Issue of Equal Access

Given that abortions are legal and that some state governments contribute to the costs incurred by some low-income women, an emerging issue may be "equal access." Forrest et al. (1979a) state that there were 2567 abortion providers in 1977—1695 hospitals, 448 nonhospital abortion clinics, and 424 physicians (an acknowledged undercount) who performed abortions in their private offices. "Although the clinics represented only 17 percent of the abortion service providers in 1976, they accounted for 62 percent of all reported abortions. In 1976, eight out of 10 public hospitals and six out of 10 non-Catholic private hospitals—a total of 3,700 hospitals—did not provide any abortion services."

Forrest et al. conclude from this that abortion services are "still much more likely to be available in larger than in smaller metropolitan areas or in non-metropolitan areas. Inaccessibility of abortion services is believed to be a major reason that some 611,780 women in need were unable to obtain abortions in 1976 and another 458,000 had to travel to another, often distant, state or county to obtain them." Poor, young, rural, and minority group women were especially disadvantaged by such inaccessibility of services.

It is difficult to foresee what impact the June 30, 1980, Supreme Court ruling will have on the equal access issue. Before that ruling, the pro-abortion forces could argue that, if abortion is legal and if government is paying for it for the poor, then government has to make abortion providers at least reasonably accessible for all because otherwise some would-be consumers are denied the opportunity to exercise their rights. Although the June 30 ruling obscures that argument, two extreme arguments are still possible, with infinite variations between.

On the pro-abortion side, it may be argued that abortions for poor and rich alike are still legal, but if inaccessibility for women in some areas makes exercising that right feasible only for the rich, then public policy is discriminatory and must be changed. The anti-abortion argument needs only to extend the June 30, 1980, Supreme Court logic. If policies equalizing accessibility are legislatively discretionary rather than constitutionally mandatory, then Congress and the state legislatures *can* decide against such policies and *should* do so. Only time will tell which arguments are furthered and which will ultimately dominate.

Discussion

A unique feature about abortion is that nobody likes it. Certainly the anti-abortion groups do not. From the consumer's point of view, it is an emotionally draining experience for all, which lasts indefinitely for some, and I know of no provider who actually enjoys performing an abortion. A common wish among these three is that the unwanted pregnancy had not occurred in the first place, but consensus ends there.

The anti-abortion side considers abortion to be a vile, sinful, murderous act of butchery. At the 1980 Baltimore White House Conference on Families, a coalition of anti-abortion groups walked out when they failed to defeat two pro-abortion recommendations. A week following that, the Southern Baptist Convention, the nation's largest Protestant body, strongly denounced abortion and called for a law to prohibit it except to save the life of the mother. Two weeks following that, the heavily religious, pro-family pro-life movement held a counter-conference in Washington, D.C., to articulate the views that had been rejected at the Baltimore White House Conference; expectedly, anti-abortion sentiment and political activism were the unifying themes for a rather diverse group.

The pro-abortion side has been equally vocal. Feminist groups reduce the argument to the right of each woman to choose her own destiny. Some professional groups define abortion services as humane and socially responsible. One such group, the American Public Health Association, has passed pro-abortion resolutions over many years. The following resolution (see the March, 1980, issue of *American Journal of Public Health,* p. 305) is its latest policy resolution and focuses on second trimester (middle months of pregnancy) abortions:

Policy Statement No. 7907: The Right to Second Trimester Abortion
The American Public Health Association,
　　Recognizing that it has consistently advocated women's right to abortion (Resolution #7626), physicians' freedom to perform abortion, and state legislation for legal abortion (#6718); and has urged the removal of state statutes restricting abortion (#7118), and supported the inclusion of abortion in public funding (#7025); and
　　Acknowledging that although the United States Supreme Court has recognized women's right to abortion to the point of viability in the 1973 *Doe vs. Wade* decision, anti-abortion groups are harassing women seeking abortions as well as abortion providers across the country, and are creating immense pressure on physicians who perform later abortion procedures; and
　　Noting that only 9 per cent of legal abortions are performed in the second trimester of pregnancy; that greater use of the Dilatation and Evacuation procedure makes it possible to perform the vast majority of second trimester abortions during or prior to the 16th week after the last menstrual period (LMP), which is the 14th week of pregnancy;[1] and that most women who seek abortions after the 16th week LMP are facing severe social and health circumstances, such as

pregnancy at a very young age or involving a fetus with known serious congenital abnormalities or disease; and

Noting that through curtailment of funding at both the federal and state levels, poor women have seen their right to abortion erode; therefore

1. Renews its support of women's right to abortion up to and including to the point of viability;

2. Urges strong opposition to local and state proposed or enacted ordinances which present misleading and nonfactual information which may be perceived to frighten and harass women who choose abortion and health care providers performing these abortions;

3. Urges endorsement of educational programs which train physicians and health care personnel to provide safe later abortion techniques of Dilatation and Evacuation and saline infusion; and

4. Urges endorsement of the provision of second trimester abortion in freestanding qualified clinics that meet the state standards required for certifications.

Reference

1. Grimes DA, et al: Mid-trimester abortion by dilatation and evacuation: a safe and practical alternative. N Engl J Med 296:1141-1145, 1977.

The consumption of abortion services, of course, has profound impact on families. It self-evidently prevents increases in family size and it prevents or delays family formation by those who might otherwise choose the shotgun marriage solution or start, by default, single-parent families.

The motivation to have an abortion has individual and family well-being inextricably intertwined. There are those who are motivated to protect their health—life- or health-threatening pregnancies and pregnancies resulting from rape or incest. For those who are not married, there is motivation to keep a job (stay in school), to delay marriage until they are ready for that responsibility, to avoid embarrassment and turmoil, or to avoid having babies they feel unable to care for. For married persons, there is motivation to prevent the loss of employment or other threats to economic stability, to avoid threats to relationship stability in the family, or to protect life-styles (e.g., premenopausal women who don't want to start the parenting cycle again at their age). The anti-abortion groups, of course, feel that none of these reasons is sufficient for terminating an embryonic human's life, except for a few dire situations.

Public policy has been caught unwillingly in the center of the conflicts—government should serve all, but the demands of the two extremes are mutually exclusive. At the moment, neither the anti-abortion groups nor the pro-abortion groups are in the ascendency. The courts have set policy by declaring abortion legal, but stating that public monies may be appropriately withheld. The legislative and executive branches have set and implemented policy in this context, principally through Title XIX of the Social Security Act—the Medicaid program. The impacts of these policies are applauded by one section of society and cursed by another. The struggle does not appear ended. It has been an important, but unpleasant, chapter in the history of American public policy.

A fuller discussion of this topic, of course, would include consideration of policy options that reduce the extent of unwanted pregnancies and policy options that soften the blow for those electing not to terminate their pregnancies, but such a consideration serves only to expand controversial issues. Policy options that would enlarge income support programs for those unable to work and care for newborn children simultaneously, thereby allowing women to carry their pregnancies to term, are not attractive to many potential consumers, and the "welfare system" is generally unpopular throughout society, especially among taxpayers. The adoption market is quantitatively inadequate for all unwanted pregnancies and is not an attractive option to the majority of women with unwanted pregnancies, judging from consumption rates. Increasing birth control availability is already a matter of public policy, but is also offensive to many of the same people who object to abortions, especially in regard to adolescents. Also, influencing sexual practices in a conservative direction implies value judgments that are not within the purview of public policy, residing instead in the private sector.

This fuller policy context of unwanted pregnancies is one of enormous import to millions of Americans and promises to occupy center stage in public debate into the foreseeable future. The narrower context of the abortion issue has been discussed above because it is probably the consummate example of a public policy issue. It is an *issue* of the first magnitude in that there are many defensible points of view about it that are irreconcilable. It is a *public policy* issue: consumers and religious groups and legal rights groups and professional societies—all from the private sector—have pressed the public sector for decisions and actions favorable to their causes. What the public sector *can* do is being decided in the judicial branch; what government *should* do is being decided in the legislative branch; implementing the "should" is the executive branch. The issue has not been resolved, nor is it likely to be in the immediate future.

DISABILITY

Disability has become such a catch-all term that Nagi (1966) found it profitable to distinguish among three concepts as a way of ordering one's understanding of the subject. Although not all disability experts subscribe to his classification scheme, it is probably the most widely accepted one and most alternative schemes are compatible with it.

Nagi differentiated among impairment, functional limitation, and disability. *Impairment* is a deviation from normal health that is generally described in medical terms—hypertension, cerebral palsy, cleft lip, gout, and so forth. A *functional limitation* is a performance deficiency that results from an impairment—loss of mobility, for example. Different impairments may cause the same functional limitation: a person's reduced mobility may result from amputation, stroke, cerebral palsy, severe emotional reactions, or various other impairments.

Disability is a condition which limits the normal performance of customary roles in life, especially vocational and familial, and a given type of disability may result from a variety of functional limitations and underlying impairments. A bus driver may be disabled because of loss of mobility due to a stroke or to loss of sight or to a variety of other limitations. A given functional limitation may not totally limit role performance of all persons having it; a 50% loss of mobility may disable a bus driver, but not a computer programmer, whose position does not require high mobility. In recent years a distinction has been made between disability resulting from a *loss* of an ability in adult life—such as the bus driver—and developmental disabilities that occur during childhood and interfere with the *acquisition* of abilities—such as a child born with a cleft lip, who may encounter difficulty acquiring normal speech.

Over the life cycle, major sets of problems are predictable. At birth, moderate to severe congenital anomalies impair about 10% of newborns. During the school years, learning requirements are such that mental deficiency, emotional disturbances, and specific learning problems may severely disable children in school. In adult life, vocational disabilities predominate, with both emotional and physical disorders underlying the disability. Among the elderly, the cumulative impact of minor and severe limitations leaves many unable to care for themselves.

All of the above is focused more on individuals than on families, even when one is disabled in a family role. We do not identify the family as "disabled" even when the mother is so psychotic that she is unable to rear her children. Data on the magnitude of disability, consequently, yield estimates of disabled individuals in the general population rather than of families with one or more disabled members. One hears estimates that one family in ten has a disabled member, but such rules of thumb do not stand under close scrutiny.

Occasionally the introduction of a disabled person into a family has a positive effect overall by creating a common challenge within the family's coping ability. However, even in those cases, no one is really grateful for the disability, and it seems reasonable to say that all cases of disability are undesired and problematical, at least to the disabled person.

The disabled person in the family may experience a variety of problems, especially emotional ones. The severely disabled veteran, for instance, may see himself as a person of little worth because he can't work and can't play catch with his son or mow the grass or lift something too heavy for his wife, and he may resent his dependence on family members for transportation to medical facilities or help with appliances. It is not difficult to imagine the types of difficulties he may experience.

Less well understood are the problems of the nondisabled members of the family. The disabled member may be a drain on their time; it takes time to provide personal care and supervision to the disabled member, to transport him to the various services he needs, to shop for him, to assume his duties in the family. The disabled member may be a drain on emotional reserves; the worry, the empathy, the struggle to keep feelings under control exact a toll over time. The disabled member may be a drain on family finances; not all services are free or covered by insurance, and sometimes family members may have to forego working to provide in-home care or supervision. The disabled person may be a drain on independent decision-making; the bread-winner may not be able to accept a promotion at work because it requires a move to a part of the state where needed services are not readily available. The cumulative impact of these drains may be a general impoverishment of the life experience for the nondisabled family members.

The relationships among the family members (disabled and nondisabled) are strained by these problems. Divorce, self-sacrifice, abuse, dedication, love, and neglect are some of the adaptive and maladaptive responses.

Throughout our history the general population has usually been supportive of government programs for the disabled since their lot in life is generally not of their own doing. The incremental growth of the service system, however, has generally been in response to this disability subgroup or that, so that the total federal effort is dispersed throughout government without central control. The following is a partial listing of federal disability programs identified by the Office for Handicapped Individuals (*Federal Assistance* . . . , 1979):

Department of Health, Education and Welfare (now Department of Health and
  Human Services)
  Health Services
      Crippled Children's Services
      Maternal and Child Health Services
  Office of Education
      Handicapped Preschool and School Programs
      Vocational Education
      Educational Innovation and Support
      Deaf-Blind Centers
      Handicapped Personnel Preparation
  Office of Human Development Services
      Vocational Rehabilitation Services
      Head Start

President's Committee on Mental Retardation
Architectural and Transportation Barriers Compliance Board
Social Security Administration
    Disability Insurance
    Supplementary Security Income
Veterans Administration
    Rehabilitation Engineering Research
    Compensation for Service-Connected Disability
    Vocational Rehabilitation
Library of Congress
    Books for the Blind and Physically Handicapped
Small Business Administration
    Handicapped Assistance Loans
Department of Labor
    Longshoremen's and Harbor Worker's Compensation
    Coal Mine Worker's Compensation

Programs that state and local governments sponsor vary considerably from place to place, as do programs in the private sector. Families that have recently gained a disabled member are frequently overwhelmed by the complexity of the service system and the pathways to service. They are well advised to contact the local association for the disability or impairment the family member has for an orientation to the service system in their area. Such associations are usually organized for specific impairments, e.g., associations for retarded children. Clergymen, social workers, and public health nurses are particularly well informed about how to locate these groups.

Although the general public has been supportive of government programs for the disabled, many elements of the service system have been resistant to change, and people have taken to the courts for redress of grievances. Parents have been particularly active on behalf of their handicapped children, especially in regard to educational needs (Abeson et al., 1975). Court decisions and pending cases had become so numerous by 1975 that the Council for Exceptional Children began an annual updating of pending and completed litigation.

More recently, the courts have assumed a dominant, but inconclusive, role relative to institutional care for the mentally retarded and mentally ill in large institutions. In a technology-poor nineteenth century environment, it became customary to place mentally retarded and mentally ill persons in institutions where they could live out their lives safely and without undue burden on their families. Mortality from periodic epidemics and other causes made room for new admissions. Following World War II, however, reduction in mortality as a result of antibiotics led to overcrowding of incredible dimensions and the demand for reform. Concurrently, technological advances in the medical control of psychiatric symptomatology, in special education, in habilitative services, in modified work environments, and in supportive therapy first made institutionalization unnecessary for many and later made it inadvisable for others. Habilitation and treatment in the community became the technologically attainable standard. The philosophy of normalization (Wolfensberger, 1970) spread from Scandinavia to this country, holding that service patterns should minimize, not maximize, the pathological part of a person's life; "warehousing" people in institutions was the antithesis of normalization. This philosophy, plus research findings that disabled persons progressed better in community than in institutional settings, led to nationwide petitions to courts to require states to deinstitutionalize those who could better profit from treatment and habilitation services in the less restrictive community. The courts, for the most part, have ruled for the plaintiffs and the resulting deinstitutionalization trend made a gruesome debut.

Many of the community facilities to which people were deinstitutionalized were worse than the institutions in terms of care, safety, and food. In some urban areas there was an early tendency to cluster the community facilities in slums, which was hardly a normalizing influence. Many persons were returned to families that were ill-prepared to care for them. Many institutions simply did not respond to court orders to deinstitutionalize. The most famous such case, the *Pennhurst* case in Pennsylvania, will be heard by the Supreme Court in the fall of 1980.

Perhaps the most profound influence of deinstitutionalization is its effects on admission rates. While resident populations continue to wait for community placement, new admissions have been reduced or eliminated altogether, leaving families with new cases necessarily dependent on community services.

In spite of its rocky start, the opinion here is that the deinstitutionalization trend will continue, forcing a division of labor on families and community-based services. The transition toward this new system of care has not been pleasant to date, and untold numbers of families may continue to experience considerable frustration and indebtedness and emotional exhaustion while the community service system builds a capacity to shoulder its share of the division of labor.

There has been a similar parallel trend for the disabled and ailing elderly. With the advent of Medicaid in the sixties, nursing homes flourished and Medicaid expenditures rose from less than $1 billion in 1967 to over $6 billion in 1977, with no downward trend in sight. The growth has truly exceeded anyone's wildest expectations, so that "cost containment" has become the obsession of policy analysts. Expectedly, the only alternative to nursing home care is the family, supported by continuing home health care services. Interestingly, the family is not considered the problem, but the solution. (See Callahan et al., 1980, for a general treatise on family care.)

Most commentaries on the American family, as stated earlier, allude to the loss of family functions to specialized institutions in society over our history. Disability is the principal exception to that trend. Science finds that the disabled do best at home or in homelike circumstances. Policy analysts find that the cost of total government care in institutions is preposterously high. Public policy, therefore, is increasingly asking the family to take the care of the disabled back on the understanding that government will assume a responsible division of labor with it. Whether this is a triumph or a tragedy for the family depends on how well government holds up its end of the bargain.

POVERTY

One wonders what remains to be said about poverty. For two decades now, the public has been bombarded with facts and dramas and policies and crises about poverty and its colleagues—racism, unemployment, urban blight, welfare inequities, crime, illegitimacy, hopelessness, high mortality, substance abuse, domestic violence, and rats. The litany of government responses is equally long—employment programs, disability insurance, welfare payments, public health activities, neighborhood organization programs, Social Security, youth employment programs, education demonstrations, community mental health centers, recreation programs, senior citizen centers, food stamps, job training programs, day care centers, food stamps, job training programs, drug abuse programs, public housing, and a host of others.

Whether the total government effort has been successful or not is a matter of personal opinion and what kind of mood one is in at the moment. Certainly we do not have in this country the pockets of half-starved, half-clothed people that many undeveloped countries do, and we would indeed have them without our programs. Yet, we still have acre after acre of the urban poor in every U.S. city—areas that most people are afraid to drive through, which suggests what kind of hell it must be to live there. The plight of the rural poor in the south, Appalachia, and the southwest seems less acute only because the density of human misery is less.

All of this is well known to everybody. The only dimension to poverty that seems not to have become common fare in the media is the international dimension, especially the contrast in democratic and communist styles. The communist appeal to the Third World is to enfranchise the disenfranchised with land reform, guaranteed employment, free medical care and, in general, a decent standard of living for all by having the same standard of living for all. It would be nice if we had a welfare system that we thought offered the disenfranchised a better deal than they could get under communism, but we really don't. Our public relations are limited to the winners in the competitive, free market. The average person, rich or poor, distrusts our welfare system, to say the least. It is not something we hold up to our communist rivals and say, "Hey, try to top this!" Instead, to the taxpayer it seems to be a bottomless pit into which we pour one ineffectual billion after another, and to the poor it seems like a band-aid solution to endemic problems in an insensitive, cruel society. William Raspberry (syndicated columnist; February 29, 1980) poses the dilemma in the public eye this way:

> There's (a) dilemma to the business of welfare. If welfare grants are set at levels high enough to provide elemental decency for recipients, they become a disincentive to work. And if they are low enough to encourage recipients to take even low-paid work, they condemn to squalor those who do not manage to find work in our job-poor economy.

Although few seem agreed on the best way to approach poverty in the decades ahead, the issue sharply divides along the line of end-of-process solutions for people in trouble and normalizing solutions. Consider the following choice. First, we could double our efforts to aid people in trouble—more psychiatrists and social workers and probation officers, more financial support for those without income, more drug treatment programs, more food stamps, and so on down the line. Or we could double our efforts to ensure jobfullness, to offer evening clinics in neighborhoods for medical care, and to make reproductive control available for those who want it, to make fair-priced shopping facilities reasonably accessible, to make home ownership more attainable, and so on down the line. Which of the two options would have the greater impact? Chances are most would opt for the normalizing influences while admitting that the end-of-process solutions cannot be reduced until the positive effects of normalization have rooted deeply—over an entire generation according to some. The first option of ameliorating the life conditions of the poor seems to most to be little more than ladling out Bower's bucket (Chapter 1) with the faucet on.

Such broad-scale solutions require more, not fewer, rationally planned government inputs. Unfortunately, at this writing the state of the economy is such that large-scale marginal increases in federal anti-poverty programs are not seen as feasible, which delays long-term solutions, inundates those programs that are trying to piece together the end-of-process problems, and treats millions of American families to a life-style in which stability and fullness are miraculous accidents.

The long-standing problem of large-scale poverty has been aggravated by large-scale inflation over the past decade. The poverty level has risen to the following levels for nonfarm families (*Federal Register,* Monday, April 21, 1980, p. 26713):

No. in family	Poverty level
1	$3790
2	5010
3	6230
4	7450
5	8670
6	9890

Yet many states have not increased their welfare payments commensurately or at all, thereby reducing subsistence support to something far less than that.

Government data on the federal effort are difficult to decipher. Table 3 provides data on federal social welfare expenditures from HEW Research and Statistics Note No. 2, Februrary 14, 1980. The total federal effort, which is 61% of social welfare efforts at all levels of government, amounted to $240 billion in 1978—an enormous total that is 11.8% of the gross national product and 55.3% of all federal expenditures. Yet, the total welfare effort as a percentage of gross national product has been declining in recent years.

Addressing the poverty issue effectively is self-evidently one of the highest priorities for family policy, and one of the least likely to succeed on the scale it deserves in the foreseeable future. Particularly disturbing is the distress currently being experienced by our liberal role models in Scandinavia. In Sweden, for example, nearly one-fourth of the population draws state pensions for old age or disability (Zanker, 1980). Although the cost of these programs has been increasing by nearly 7% per year, the economy has grown by less than 2% annually, with a projected budget deficit of 13.6 billion dollars—over 11% of the country's output. The per capita tax burden of $5600 (twice that of the U.S.) has become so onerous that wholesale taxpayer strikes are feared. For the first time in decades, large-scale reductions in social programs are being seriously considered to protect the economy and the taxpayer.

Probably the next major effort to reduce the extent of poverty will focus on jobfullness because that is consistent with the taxpayer's "make 'em

Table 3.   Total federal social welfare expenditures as a percentage of gross national product and federal government expenditures for all purposes, 1950-1978[a]

	Total federal social welfare expenditures (in millions)	Total federal social welfare as a percentage of:	
		Gross national product	Federal government expenditures for all purposes
1950	$10,541	4.0%	26.2%
1955	14,623	3.9	22.3
1960	24,957	5.0	28.1
1965	37,712	5.7	32.6
1970	77,337	8.1	40.1
1975	167,470	11.5	54.0
1976	197,355	12.1	57.1
1977	218,514	11.9	56.3
1978[b]	240,453	11.8	55.3

[a]Data are taken from HEW Research and Statistics Note No. 2, February 14, 1980.
[b]Provisional data.

work" philosophy and because research has recently begun to show how broadly devastating job*less*ness is. Brenner (1976), for instance, correlated the employment rate with several "social stress indicators" and found the following cumulative percentage of change in indicator incidences for a 1.4% rise in unemployment:

Suicide	5.7%
State mental hospital admission	4.7
State prison admission	5.6
Homicide	8.06
Cirrhosis of the liver mortality	2.7
Cardiovascular-renal disease	2.7
Total mortality	2.7

Clearly, relative to the concept of Bower's bucket, large-scale joblessness must be shut off before ladling efforts can take effect. Not doing so is not only illogical, but cruel.

Poverty is an unpopular issue of immense importance for which no short-run solution exists and no long-run plan seems ready for adoption. Probable failure in this area makes all other family policy options that much weaker.

HOME MORTGAGE RATES

As a picture can save a thousand words, so can a case example. There was an interesting little scandal about the mayor of the District of Columbia on the front page of the *Washington Star* in the fall of 1979. Shortly after the mayor's wife had been appointed a director of a local savings and loan association, they purchased a rather modest home in the city and assumed a 30-year, $100,000 mortgage on it—not unusual in the expensive housing market in the nation's capital. Consistent with the savings and loan association's policy for directors and executives, they were granted a 8.75% interest rate rather than the prevailing 12%, which immediately caught the eye of the media.

The front-page story provided the following data to illustrate just how much this interest break would benefit the mayor and his wife each month, each year, and for the total 30 years:

	8.75%	12%	Difference
Monthly	$ 786.70	$ 1,028.61	$ 241.91
Yearly	$ 9,440.41	$ 12,343.35	$ 2,902.94
30 years	$283,212.18	$370,300.56	$87,088.38

The difference that less than 4% makes is fascinating; over the 30-year period, nearly $90,000 is saved. More interesting is the total cost of the $100,000 mortage over 30 years. At 8.75%, the mayor invests $100,000 in his home and $183,000 in the bank; at 12%, he still invests $100,000 in his home, but he contributes $270,000 to the bank—more than a quarter million dollars!

Since that time, housing costs have continued upward, so that it is not unusual at all for middle-income families to project a lifetime home investment of a quarter to a third of a million dollars, or higher, with most of that going to the bank—for rather modest housing. Since many American families, especially young and middle-age ones, move periodically and the early years of mortgage payments are predominantly to the bank's interest than to the family's principal, the total lifetime commitment to housing costs is gargantuan, with rather small returns for the family. Such a system protects the banking enterprise, the construction enterprise, and the building materials enterprise, with the family paying continuously over its lifetime.

The options available to families are not enticing. They can rent an apartment or downscale their housing expectations; a skilled, knowledgeable few can build their own homes; or they can commit a large proportion of their lifetime earnings for housing commensurate with their aspirations, hoping that promotions at work and inflation adjustments to their pay will ease the burden a little with time.

Although interest rates on all borrowing are also up, the problem is not quite so acute there since there is the alternative of saving for interest-free cash purchases for those with the income and discipline to do so. Housing, however, is most needed in the earlier years of marriage when children are growing up, which forces the young couple to commit its early, smaller earnings for ample quarters, although they will be better able to afford them when the children are grown, earnings are highest, and space needs less ample. So they are caught.

FLEXITIME

Flexitime, called Variable Working Hours by some, is an employee-management arrangement wherein the employee is granted some control over the hours he/she works. It typically employs a "core" time, such as 9 A.M. to 3 P.M., during which all employees must work, and a "bandwidth," such as 7 A.M. to 6 P.M., during which approved employees fill in their hours to the customary limit, usually 40 hours per week.

Flexitime originated at the Messerschmidt Research and Development Center near Munich, Germany, in 1967 and spread rapidly throughout Europe in the 1960s (Langholz, 1972). Management took the initiative for its development in the context of a scarce labor supply in which flexitime was viewed as an aid in recruiting and holding personnel. It spread to the U.S. in the early 1970s and has been generally well received by both government and private industry. An attempt to assess the magnitude of its use was made in the 1980 Census, with findings due shortly.

The variations in the basic flexitime model are seemingly infinite. The core time can be expanded or reduced as feasibility dictates, as can the surrounding band of time to as little as 30 minutes on either side of the core or to as large as sound management permits. A given employee may stay permanently on, say, an early arrive/early leave schedule or vary it daily. Credits and debits for hours worked or not worked can aggregate and be balanced weekly or monthly to an agreed-upon total. Some units in large organizations may have more flexibility than others.

The system works better with white collar than with blue collar workers and with lower-level workers than higher. Employees generally seem happy with the arrangement; they are better able to meet obligations such as getting the children to school or handling emergencies at home, and are better able to shop and consume services at otherwise inconvenient hours. Those who want it can avoid some of the commuter crunch or fit into a car pool with people on different work hours. This, in turn, has a broader benefit of easing peak-hour traffic jams.

Management has been generally satisfied. Staff morale improves, and tardiness and absenteeism are reduced. Since many employees are willing to work late to complete a job so that they can get compensatory leave at a convenient time later, efficiency is better and overtime is reduced. Turnover may also be reduced. Not all findings are positive, however (Hedges, 1977). Variable schedules do produce occasional problems in communication, supervision, and workflow, and the generally longer work day may result in higher heating and lighting bills.

A more important problem is organized labor's failure to support flexitime experiments, opting instead for advocating a shorter workweek. Owen (1977) cites a British experience as an example of labor's concern. Workers in one firm there routinely worked four hours overtime on Wednesday evenings because of a peak mid-week demand, but were relatively idle on Mondays and Fridays. When flexitime was introduced, most workers chose to take compensatory time on Monday or Friday to have a long weekend. Labor officials argued that the workers benefited from such arrangements less than management. Although the workers do get some control over their time and get the longer weekends they want, management gets the same job done while saving overtime pay; the more continuously intense work hours of the employees are not rewarded with a higher hourly wage. Also, the generally more attractive work hours might incline more to enter the work force, swelling it in some places beyond the available jobs.

It does appear that flexitime is here to stay, although no one knows how extensive its use has become or what its maximum potential is. The federal government is the nation's largest employer and flexitime experiments in such bureaus as the Department of Commerce may spread throughout the federal government and to state and local governments. Additionally, the idea is beginning to appeal to those policy analysts who wonder whether its widespread use will constitute an alternative to expensive day care programs pre- and postwork, and whether part-time variations of flexitime to coincide with school hours might liberate some women with children to earn needed money without having to reinvest it in child care arrangements.

The key element of flexitime from a family policy perspective is that it gives some control of work hours to family members so that they can better balance some of the conflicting demands of work and home, a remarkable achievement in an era of increasing bureaucratic controls.

ENERGY, FOOD, AND SELF-SUFFICIENCY

Every single American has been touched by the energy crisis through the jump in the price of gas, home fuel, fertilizer, and all products derived from petroleum. Adaptive responses range from the family to the federal government; families have lowered their thermostats, purchased smaller cars, cut wood, and generally reduced the demand for petroleum; the federal government has offered tax incentives for home conservation efforts, underwritten the initial cost of developing synthetic fuels and alternatives such as solar energy, and invested heavily in diplomatic efforts to protect the sources of our imported oil. Self-sufficiency is the principle at stake; since we no longer are self-sufficient with regard to energy, our policy options are 1) to stabilize a mutually dependent relationship with oil-exporting countries and/or 2) to develop alternative forms of energy that will return us to self-sufficiency as a nation.

Less well known is the food crisis, because we are still a world leader in agricultural output. However, it is a chilling experience to read Lester Brown's *The Twenty-Ninth Day* (1978); the world's four main biological systems—the oceans, grasslands, forests, and croplands—have already been overused to a degree that spells impending calamity. The principle at stake is the self-sufficiency of the entire world for food production. That massive food shortages in parts of the world are already here is evident from a reading of the report from the Presidential Commission on World Hunger, *Overcoming World Hunger: The Challenge Ahead* (1980).

Self-sufficiency is probably the heart of all public policy (see Chapter 7), and family well-being and self-sufficiency obviously cannot be considered in isolation of all the other interlocking dimensions of society. In this regard one can agree with Johnson et al. (1978) that we already have innumerable family-relevant policies, and with Kamerman (1976) that one of the principal tasks at hand is to link these policies more deliberately and constructively to family well-being and self-sufficiency. By extension, it seems that those who argue that public policy should leave the family alone are uninformed or have a narrow definition of public policy or are simply irresponsible.

PERSONAL EXPERIENCES AND THE JAUNDICED EYE

Government has grown to the degree that everyone experiences contact with it regularly, and not all of the contacts are rewarding—many leave persons disillusioned, hurt, angry, and embittered. One embittered man took the time to ventilate his feelings in the Sunday magazine section of the *Baltimore Sun* (June 15, 1980, p. 20):

> A few years ago my wife and I toured the submarine USS Torsk, moored in the Inner Harbor. For double the standard admission, we purchased brass tokens to be used as lifetime free passes to revisit the submarine.
>
> The other day I went to see the Torsk again. Although I had my original token, it cost me $1.50 to get on board. The woman at the ticket booth explained that, since my last visit, the city had purchased the sub from the state and would not honor the tokens issued by the state.
>
> This episode, though not a major catastrophe, is just one more instance of government unilaterally and capriciously "changing the rules" to suit its needs and interests. Essentially, governments today serve only their own self-perpetuating interests, and we, the people, have little to say about it.

An interesting feature of this man's complaint is that he generalized from his experience to government as a whole, which reflects both a high standard of expected performance and an accumulation of negative personal experiences reinforced by the experiences of others.

A recent survey of "trust" by the *Ladies' Home Journal* (October, 1980) of 1000 of its readers suggests that this man's statement reflects a generally jaundiced view of society. The respondents estimated the increase or decrease of trust they had experienced over the past decade for selected institutions:

+60	God
+ 2	Computers
− 7	Doctors
− 9	TV news coverage
−29	Drug manufacturers
−35	Appliance manufacturers
−39	Newspapers
−40	Food manufacturers
−41	Aircraft manufacturers
−41	Economists
−48	Advertising
−54	U.S. courts
−55	The President
−60	Nuclear power plant operators
−64	State government
−71	Auto manufacturers
−81	Congress

Additionally, the readers were asked to identify their most trusted newscasters, TV stars, writers or columnists, religious leaders, and political leaders. For all categories except newscasters, "none" was the modal response; for newscasters, Walter Cronkite out-polled "none" by 40% to 31%.

Clearly this represents a jaundiced view of society. With the exception of God and Walter Cronkite, these middle-class women reported a declining sense of trust in the world around them. Whether this represents an accurate perception of the world or a painful transition from fantasy to more realistic expectations or something else is a matter of conjecture, but it should be pointed out that four of the bottom six categories above are "government."

Rightly or wrongly, therefore, the trustworthiness of government has become an issue unto itself for many persons.

MISCELLANEOUS

Some issues are unmistakably family-oriented in nature. Divorce is the prime example because it implies the dissolution of the principal relationship within the family. Other issues focus on both individuals and families, in roughly equal parts. Substance abuse, for instance, is becoming in the eyes of many the most pressing individual and family problem in America. The disastrous effects of alcoholism are well documented, and the grotesque experience of having a drug-dependent adolescent in a family is approaching epidemic proportions. Treatment of the troubled individual in a family context has become the norm.

Still other family issues are intergenerational in nature. Filial responsibility is a good example: as more couples live till the golden years, they die slowly from chronic diseases in contrast to quicker deaths in earlier years and in earlier times because of communicable diseases, heart attacks, accidents, and formerly untreatable diseases. The costs and time demands resulting from this situation strain intergenerational relationships, and the magnitude of the problem will increase as the post–World War II baby boom approaches the retirement years.

DISCUSSION

Abortion is one of the better examples of the *diversity of policy actors*. All three branches of government participate, as do members of the scientific/ professional community in both the public and private sectors, advocacy groups pro and con, religious groups, private citizens, and provider organizations.

Abortion and disability compare and contrast along several dimensions. In terms of *unit of conceptualization,* both focus primarily on the individual, but both have strong, obvious family implications. In terms of *trends in dominance,* both have experienced an increasing reliance on the courts for direction and redress of grievances. In terms of *centrality of implementation* of policy, abortions have traditionally been funded mainly through one program, Medicaid, with one legislative base, Title XIX of the Social Security Act; disability, on the other hand, is approached through diverse programs emanating from diverse legislation. In terms of *policy consensus,* there is none for abortions nor will there be in the near future; for disability, there is considerable consensus on the appropriateness of governmental action and there seems to be emerging consensus that family care should receive increasing priority over institutional care. In terms of *policy objectives,* policy on abortions is focused on rule-setting for what people can and cannot do in this society and whether government will underwrite the costs. For disability, policy is focused on formulating service strategies for ameliorating the life circumstances of the handicapped. Both disability and abortion are considered to be *important,* and both have *attainable objectives.*

Some policy issues do well along one dimension and poorly along another. Poverty is considered to be important, but many believe that our goals relative to it are not attainable with current resources, and marginally increasing resources does not seem feasible while the economy is down. In terms of *public–private sector relationships,* flexitime and home mortgages are primarily the business of the private sector, but are influenced by government action and inaction. In terms of *scope of the problem,* energy and food prices exist on an international scale and solutions must be on that level. Finally, in terms of *efficiency of problem solving,* government as a whole is currently experiencing a credibility problem in the eyes of many.

The dimensions of family public policy mentioned above are not an exhaustive list, but they seem to illustrate the breadth and complexity of the topic and provide a perspective for viewing the press for family-relevant policies in the 1980s.

Abortion Consent Procedures for Adolescents, State by State

State	Child's consent sufficient	Parental notice requirement	Comments
Alabama	No—parent's consent	None	By Dr. in approved hosp.; 30 day residence requirement
Alaska	No—parent's consent	None	30 day residence requirement; by Dr. or surgeon
Arizona	Statute refers to *Belloti* v. *Baird,* 418 U.S. 132 (1976)		
Arkansas	No—parent's written consent	None	4 month residence requirement; only in hospital
California	Yes (refers to *Ballard* v. *Anderson,* 4 c. 3d 873 (1971)	None	Therapeutic abortion, in accredited hospital
Colorado	No—parent's consent	None	Only therapeutic abortion
Connecticut	Declared unconstitutional. See: *Abele* v. *Morkle* (D. Conn. 1973) 369 F. Supp. 807, 423 U.S. 9		
Delaware	Yes—minor 12 or older	Discretionary with doctor, primary consideration minor's best interest	Only therapeutic abortions
District of Columbia	Minor not specifically mentioned	None	Only therapeutic abortions
Florida	Yes	Good faith effort	Dr. in approved facility
Georgia	Minor not specifically mentioned	None	Dr. says necessary; no abortion after 2nd trimester except save life mother
Hawaii	Minor not specifically mentioned but see Sect. 577A-1	None	Dr. must perform, in hospital if after 2nd trimester
Idaho	Yes	None	Minor cannot be forced to abort
Illinois	No—parent's consent (if refused have court order)	None	Dr. decides in best judgment have abortion
Indiana	Yes	None	

(continued)

State	Child's consent sufficient	Parental notice requirement	Comments
Iowa	Yes	None	During 1st 12 weeks of pregnancy
Kansas	Yes, if Dr. believes woman needs abortion	None	
Kentucky	Yes. Statue requiring consent parent after 1st trimester held unconstitutional in *Wolfe* v. *Shroering* 541 F. 2d 523	None	
Louisiana	Yes, if 16 or older	24 hr. (72 constructive)	
Maine	Yes	24 hr.	
Maryland	Yes, if capable of informed consent or by court order	*See note a*	Cannot force minor to accept abortion
Massachusetts	Yes, if minor is mature or in best interests (*Bellotti* v. *Baird*)		
Michigan	Yes	None	Dr. must file confidential report, include age of woman
Minnesota	Yes, if emancipated	Dr. must notify parents as to why recommended abortion	
Mississippi	Statute refers to *Roe* v. *Wade,* 410 U.S. 113 & *Doe* v. *Bolton,* 410 U.S. 179		
Missouri	Yes, if emancipated or court has ordered		
Montana	Yes	Written notice if minor under 18 or unmarried except if abortion needed to save woman's life	Cannot force woman to have an abortion
Nebraska	Yes, must consult with parents	None	
Nevada	Yes, if emancipated or married (if married need husband's consent)	None	Done by Dr; in hosp. only after 1st trimester
New Hampshire	Minor not specifically mentioned	None	Only therapeutic abortions

(continued)

State	Child's consent sufficient	Parental notice requirement	Comments
New Jersey	Statute states precedent established by U.S. Supreme Court must be followed by the lower courts		
New Mexico	No—consent living parent	None	In accredited hospital
New York			
North Carolina	No. See Atty Gen. Op. 41 NCAG 489 (1971); 41 NCAG 709 (1972)	None	By Dr. in certified hospital or clinic within 20 weeks
North Dakota	Yes	Before period viability 24 hr. notice (or 48 hr. written notice) before if minor is unemancipated; after viability and to save life mother need parent consent any unmarried minor under 18	Cannot force woman to have abortion
Oklahoma	Statute refers to *Bellotti* v. *Baird*		
Oregon	No—parent's written consent except to save mother's life	None	Abortion only to: save mother; child has defect; rape
Pennsylvania	No—unless save life mother	None	Cannot force woman to abort; statute refers to *Planned Parenthood* v. *Fitzpatrick* 401 F. Supp. 554 (1975) affirmed, 428 U.S. 901
Rhode Island	Abortion statutes held unconstitutional because *Roe* v. *Wade* 410 U.S. 113 (1976)	None	No mention minor but states killing quick child is manslaughter
South Carolina	Yes but if minor 16 or younger except to save mother's life	None	
South Dakota	Yes. Statute refers to *Planned Parenthood* v. *Danforth* 428 U.S. 52 (1976)		

(continued)

State	Child's consent sufficient	Parental notice requirement	Comments
Tennessee	Yes	Notice needed unless abortion needed to save mother's life or minor is married	Parent objection not change minor's decision
Utah	Yes (Dr. must give woman name 2 adoption agencies and tell her consequences/details abortion)	If possible—Dr. consider age, family situation, minor's physical, emotional, psychological safety	
Vermont		None	
Virgin Islands	Yes	Dr. may notify parents with or without minor's consent	
Virginia	No—written parent's consent	None	Dr. must perform
Texas	No laws related to abortion per se Op. Attn. Gen. 1974 No. H-139. Proposed legislation must conform to *Roe* v. *Wade*.		
Washington	No—parent's consent But see, *State* v. *Koome* 84 Wn. 2d 901, 530 P 2d 260 (1975) holding requirement unconstitutional		
West Virginia	Statute does not specifically mention minors	None	
Wisconsin	Statute only allows therapeutic abortion; held unconstitutional. Refers to *Bellotti* v. *Baird* and *Planned Parenthood* v. *Danforth*		
Wyoming	Yes	None	No abortion after viability except save mother's life

Reprinted from: *Legal Status of Adolescents*. Scientific Analysis Corporation, San Francisco, 1980, a contract report to the U.S. Department of Health and Human Services.

[a] No notice is needed where minor lives apart from parents or reasonable efforts to notify are unsuccessful. Doctor may waive notice where believe lead to physical or mental abuse of minor.

Chapter 4

The 1980 White House Conference on Families

What happens when the President of the United States calls for a major convocation of people to discuss the American family, to discuss the family's strengths and weaknesses, and to consider how public policy affects families for better or worse? When conferences and hearings are called in every state for all interested persons to ventilate their feelings about the family and to elect delegates to the national convocation, what types of people show up and what do they say and what do they recommend? When the state delegates arrive at the national convocation, what happens—consensus or bickering or outright warfare? What recommendations result from such a convocation—pious pronouncements or hard-nosed policy options? What happens to the recommendations when they are delivered to the federal bureaucracy—ho-hum absorption into the massive and insensitive "system" or effective integration into the policymaking machine? What scandals arise during this process; what rifts in public opinion; what kinds of in-fighting?

The answers to these questions define the White House Conference on Families, promised by President Carter during his 1976 presidential campaign, administered by a small staff in the federal bureaucracy, and participated in by well over 100,000 Americans from all walks of life during 1979 and 1980. It was one of the more fascinating processes in this latter half of the twentieth century and warrants a detailed consideration because history will probably show that it elevated family public policy to a permanent spot in the public policy process.

GUIDING PHILOSOPHY, ORGANIZATION, AND OBJECTIVES

The President's Guiding Philosophy

"The main purpose of this White House Conference will be to examine the strengths of American Families, the difficulties they face and the ways in which family life is affected by public policies.'' Of all President Carter's statements about the White House Conference on Families (WHCF), this January, 1978, declaration was the one most frequently quoted throughout the WHCF process.

The President elaborated on this capsule of philosophy at the July 20, 1979, reception for the 40-member National Advisory Committee of the WHCF. Some excerpts:

> The purpose of the Family Conference . . . will be not to set up some big new expensive Federal program; it is to see what we can do, not simply as a government, but as a nation, to strengthen American families. In some instances this may mean just getting Government out of the way.

> For couples who married in the early years of this century, one marriage in ten ended in divorce; for couples who have married since World War II, one marriage in three ends in divorce. The rate of teenage suicide has doubled in the last ten years. Half a million youngsters each year run away from home. Too many of our older people are lonely and sometimes even afraid. Without question, the American family is in trouble.

> These problems I have described to you so briefly are real, but they are also the kinds of problems that families have always specialized in solving. Families, as you well know, are more than just households. They are a network of relationships rooted not only in kinship based on blood, but a kinship based on shared experiences, shared joys and sorrows and I think, most of all, shared love.

WHCF Organization

To provide overall governance and direction for WHCF activities within the context of the President's guiding philosophy, a 40-member National Advisory Committee was appointed: one chairperson, five deputy chairpersons, and 34 members. Some profiles:

Chairperson: Jim Guy Tucker, Little Rock, Arkansas; a U.S. Congressman from 1977 to 1979, he is currently a partner in the law firm of Tucker and Stafford.

Deputy chairpersons:

Mario M. Cuomo, New York, New York; Lieutenant Governor of New York

Guadalupe Gibson, San Antonio, Texas; Associate Professor of the Worden School of Social Service

Coretta Scott King, Atlanta, Georgia; President of the Martin Luther King Center for Social Change

Maryann Mahaffey, Detroit, Michigan; President Pro Tem of the Detroit City Council and Professor in the Wayne State School of Social Work

Donald V. Seibert, New York, New York; Chairman and Chief Executive Officer of the J.C. Penny Company, Inc.

The 35 members represented various components of the business, academic, religious, professional, and consumer communities. The paid staff, volunteers, and "loaners" from both the public and private sectors were under the supervision of the Executive Director of the WHCF, John L. Carr, formerly Education Director of the Campaign for Human Development, an anti-poverty funding program.

The total budget for the WHCF was $3 million.

Themes and Objectives

To develop the President's philosophy, the National Advisory Committee identified the following six themes as starting points upon which further discussion would be based.

Family strengths and supports. The family is the oldest, most fundamental human institution, our most precious national resource. Families serve as a source of strength and support for their members and our society.

Diversity of families. American families are pluralistic in nature. Our discussion of issues will reflect an understanding and respect of cultural, ethnic and regional differences as well as differences in structure and lifestyle.

The changing realities of family life. American society is dynamic, constantly changing. The roles of families and individual family members are growing, adapting and evolving in new and different ways to meet the challenges in our age.

The impact of public and private institutional policies. The policies of government and major private institutions have profound effects on families. Increased sensitivity to the needs of families is needed, as well as ongoing research and action to address the negative impact of public and private institutional policies.

The impact of discrimination. Many families are exposed to various and diverse forms of discrimination. These can affect individual family members as well as the family unit as a whole.

Families with special needs. Certain families have special needs and these needs often produce unique strengths. The needs of families with handicapped members, single-parent families, elderly families and many other families with special needs will be addressed during the Conference.

The National Advisory Committee also adopted the following eight goals for its activities:

1. To initiate broad nationwide discussions of families in the United States.
2. To develop a process of listening to and involving families themselves, especially those families which have too often been left out of the formulation of policies which affect their lives.
3. To share what is known about families—their importance, diversity, strengths, problems, responses to a changing world, etc.—and to generate and share new knowledge about families.
4. To identify public policies, institutional actions and other factors which may harm or neglect family life, as well as their differing impact on particular groups, and to recommend new policies designed to strengthen and support families.

5. To stimulate and encourage a wide variety of activities in neighborhoods, grass-roots organizations, communities, states, national organizations, media, and other public and private groups focused on supporting and strengthening families and individuals within families.

6. To examine the impact of economic forces (poverty, unemployment, inflation, etc.) on families, with special emphasis and involvement of poor families.

7. To encourage diverse groups of families to work together through local, state and national networks and other institutions for policies which strengthen and support family life.

8. To generate interest in and action on Conference recommendations among individuals, families, governmental and non-governmental bodies at every level. (These activities will include monitoring and evaluation efforts.)

Published comments by Jim Guy Tucker, NAC chairperson, and John Carr, WHCF Executive Director, consistently reinforced several points, probably reflecting those parts of the philosophy of the conference that needed frequent reinterpretation and defense. They stressed the need for pluralism in an ''open'' conference: no point of view was unwelcome and no position was favored—all were invited to participate. They stressed that the WHCF was not a forum for professional groups and advocates alone; they were particularly interested in hearing from families directly.

SKELETON PLAN

The skeleton plan of the WHCF called for a massive network of activities spanning the period of September, 1979, to March, 1981, the climax of which was to be three, rather than the usual one, White House conferences in June and July, 1980, in Baltimore, Minneapolis, and Los Angeles. The planned activities clustered into four sequential stages.

Preconference Activities

Four independent efforts from September, 1979, through March, 1980, were planned as lead-ins to the summer White House conferences.

1. National hearings, fall of 1979. To provide background material for the delegates to the summer conferences, five national hearings were planned for families to share their concerns, ideas, successes and problems with contemporary American life:
   Kansas City and Linsborg, Kansas—September 28 and 29, 1979
   Nashville, Tennessee—October 12 and 13, 1979
   Denver, Colorado—October 26 and 27, 1979
   Hartford, Connecticut—November 16 and 17, 1979
   Washington, D.C.—November 30 and December 1, 1979

2. State activities, September, 1979, through March, 1980. All 50 states and seven territories were invited to appoint state coordinators to sponsor one or more convocations in each state, the results of which would be issues and recommendations to the delegates to the summer conferences, and to oversee the process in each state for selecting delegates to the summer 1980 WHCF. The state activities would constitute the largest single set of activities in the entire WHCF process.
3. National organization activities, September, 1979, through February, 1980. Because of their expertise, it was decided to work with national organizations in several ways to concentrate the collective wisdom of the scientific community.
4. Issue work groups, October, 1980, through February, 1980.

The White House Conference on Families

The three meetings of the WHCF were scheduled for Baltimore (June 5–7, 1980) for the eastern states, Minneapolis (June 19–21) for the central states, and Los Angeles (July 10–12) for the western states. It was anticipated that approximately 650 persons would attend each of the conferences, primarily delegates from the states but supplemented with a small number of at-large delegates appointed by the conference chairperson. Members of the NAC would be full conference participants, but the small number of invited official observers would be limited in the extent of their participation.

National Task Force

In August of 1980, an ad hoc national task force would convene to identify and highlight areas of agreement in the conferences and to attempt a reconciliation of differences. It would include members of the National Advisory Committee, one representative from each state, and 20 Presidential appointees.

Implementation of Recommendations

Beginning in September, 1980, there would be a six-month implementation period as the final effort of the WHCF. Activities in this stage would include a report to the President, meetings with key federal agencies and Congressional leaders, and distribution of conference recommendations.

IMPLEMENTATION: PRECONFERENCE ACTIVITIES

National Hearings

The turnout at the first three hearings was greater than expected: 250 in Kansas and Tennessee and 870 in Denver. In all three the dominant characteristic was diversity of opinion. The November, 1979, WHCF newsletter describes the Tennessee hearing this way: "There was an enormous range of viewpoints on many subjects including the adverse impact of inflation, joblessness, racial discrimination and poverty on family life. People spoke out on religious values and families, abortion, family violence, alcoholism and other issues related to American families." In addition to the original five national hearings, two more were planned—Detroit (December 7 and 8, 1979) and Seattle (January 11 and 12, 1980).

At the end of the national hearings, several conclusions seemed warranted. First, interest in the family was intense and widespread; over 2000 persons from private citizens to U.S. Senators had testified. Second, the number of issues raised was enormous. Third, some issues were of general concern, such as inflation; some issues defied consensus, such as abortion; and some issues were regional in nature or applied only to a well-defined subpopulation, such as small farm families.

Here are some capsule summaries of testimony from various WHCF newsletters.

> Claudia Jackson, who runs a 720 acre farm with her husband in Howell, Michigan, felt it was "strange that our government should have a tax structure that penalizes (the) family."
> The carryover basis provision on inheritance taxes "threatens to place extreme hardship on small property and business owners, and imposes an almost impossible record-keeping burden on nearly every taxpaying American," she claimed, noting that "one-fourth of all farm land presently sold is sold to meet inheritance taxes. Most of the land sold limits agricultural production and the remaining farm is often too small to be a viable unit. . . . We urge our government to repeal the tax and remove the inequities."

> James A. Bergman, New England regional Director of Legal Research and Services for the Elderly, Boston, Massachusetts, reported that "some elders are beaten, starved or threatened by their children. Some are pitifully neglected, left to fend for themselves with half a Social Security check or are deprived of adequate food or medication."

> Virginia Gresham, who had moved to a small town in Kansas with her husband and three chilren, told how lonely she and her family felt after the move. "Everything really started going downhill for us," she said. "My husband was out of work. Rent payments were overdue and bills were mounting up. Everything was looking bad. It seemed we were always looking for help but couldn't find any." But finally help did come from a worker in the federally funded Community Action Program of North East Kansas.

> From the corporate side, Dick Connor, a vice-president of Control Data Corporation, reported that his company is effectively implementing a number of programs that support family viability, including flexible hours, part-time and split-time jobs, day care programs, and preemployment or "Fair Break" programs. "We have found that by helping to improve family stability through such programs, productivity is significantly improved," Connor, a member of the Minnesota Governor's Task Force on the Family, stated.

Mrs. Gloria Hudgins of Nashville discussed the problems of youth, particularly high school students who are illiterate. "When marijuana is being used on an epidemic scale, and learning is being impaired by the THC in marijuana, how can they learn?" she asked. "Why hasn't the Surgeon General issued a statement on the dangers of smoking marijuana?"

State Activities

The 50 states and seven territories were invited to appoint coordinators of state activities and all did. To aid both the states and national organizations, the National Advisory Committee developed a "Sample Topic Outline" (see Table 4). The state coordinators were convened for instruction on the spectrum of state activities, which required minimally:

1. Formation of broad-based, representative state planning committees.
2. Development of a state plan of activities including, at a minimum, a statewide conference for topic discussion and policy formulation, program and strategy recommendations as outlined in WHCF guidelines.
3. Creation and followthrough of a clear and well-publicized plan for delegate selection to the WHCF.
4. Stimulation and provision of assistance to privately sponsored activities supporting the WHCF, such as community media events, hearings, and local conferences.
5. Reporting the results of state activities to the WHCF in a uniform format.

Two of the principal outcomes of these activities were to have been the selection of ten topics of paramount concern to the participants in each state and the drafting of policy recommendations.

The process for selecting delegates from each state to the summer WHCF required a combination of gubernatorial appointment and peer election, with a minimum of 30% of the delegates being identified by each method. Each state was required to develop an affirmative action plan to ensure adequate representation of racial and ethnic groups, men and women, handicapped individuals, low-income families, and "diverse family forms." Gubernatorial appointments were to take place after peer selections and were to ensure that "the diversity and pluralism of states' families are represented in the delegation."

State Conferences

State activities, especially statewide conferences and hearings, began for some states in September, 1979, and continued into March, 1980, for others. When they were over, approximately 100,000 persons had testified—a number far in excess of projections, reflecting the intense and widespread interest in the topic throughout the country.

Table 4. Sample Topic Outline, WHCF

Themes:
Family Strengths and Supports
Diversity of Families
The Changing Realities of Family Life

The Impact of Public and Private Institutional Policies
The Impact of Discrimination
Special Needs of: Elderly Families
    Families with Handicapped Members
    Single Parent Families
    Other Families with Special Needs

Families and economic well-being	Families: challenges and responsibilities	Families and human needs	Families and major institutions
Poverty/Inadequate Income	**The Growth and Care of . . .**	**Health**	**Government-local, state, federal**
	—the child	—relationship between	—overall family perspectives
Employment/Unemployment/Under-	—the youth	families and health	—sensitivity to families
employment	—the adult	care system	—access
	—the aged	—availability, quality and	—accountability to families
Inflation		cost of health care	—military
	Marriage	—maternal and infant health	
	—preparation for marriage	—family planning	**Media**
Families and The Workplace	—supports for marriage	—mental health	—radio/t.v.
—career planning	—divorce/separation	—health education	—newspapers/magazines
—part-time, full-time, flexitime	—counseling/therapy	—drug and alcohol abuse	—movies
—transfer policies		—food and nutrition	
—sick leave and other	**Children and Parents**	—preventive care	**Law**
leave policies	—preparation for parenting	—chronic illness	—divorce/separation/alimony
—maternity leave, paternity	—supports for parents and	—long-term care	—adoption/foster care
leave	children	**Education**	—custody/child support/visitation
—increased participation in	—adoption/foster care	—availability of quality	—juvenile justice/delinquency
workforce	—parent-child relations	education	—children and the law
—counseling facilities at work	—responsible parenting	—cost of education	—child neglect/child abuse
—job sharing			

Families as Consumers
—credit
—advertising
—retail practices

Tax Policy
—marriage penalty
—child care deductions
—exemptions for dependents

Financial Assistance
—welfare and welfare reform
—food stamps
—social security
—unemployment insurance

Insurance and Pensions

Special Challenges
—handicapping conditions
—single parenthood

Family Crises
—adolescent pregnancy
—divorce
—family divorce
—death and dying
—displaced homemaker
—juvenile delinquency

Extended Family & Other Family Networks

Education (*continued*)
—home-school relations
—family life education
—special education and families
—continuing education
—sensitivity to family forms
—career education
—retraining

Housing
—availability of family housing
—cost of housing
—housing discrimination
—neighborhood and community impact
—housing displacement

Child Care
—availability of quality child care
—variety of choices: family, community, private, publicly-supported
—cost of child care

Care of the Elderly
—availability of quality care
—variety of choices: family, community, private, publicly-supported
—costs

Law (*continued*)
—court-related counseling
—spouse abuse

Social Services
—availability/accountability
—cost
—government funding: Title XX
—dissemination of information
—helping professions

Community Institutions
—self-help groups
—religions and cultural organizations
—informal supports
—civic and fraternal organizations

Philanthropy and the Voluntary Sector

Business and Industry

Transportation

I had the opportunity to attend five state conferences: three in Maryland, one in Pennsylvania, and one in Delaware. The first one, at Hood College in Frederick, Maryland, allocated the attendees to several small rooms to hear testimony. The first three in my room were:

> A woman who identified herself as a parent and challenged the right of the state to give teenagers contraceptives without parental knowledge or permission. Ditto abortions. She said the state was two-faced in its policy. It would provide contraceptives or abortions without parental knowledge or consent, but it will require the parents to accept responsibility for the costs of any complications including, God forbid, burial expenses. She said it was ridiculous that the state forbids teenagers to get their ears pierced without parental consent, but it's OK to get an abortion on their own.

> A military wife (about 55) gave a resumé of her career and concluded that it had been fun and she would do it over again. However, the frequent moves had left her without the security of a pension and, because of her age, it was becoming increasingly difficult to get new employment after each move.

> A very serious young man listed six areas he thought government could help families with: 1) teaching and education, 2) career development, 3) financial stability (especially tax structure), 4) home production, 5) physical health, and 6) social/emotional/spiritual development.

The next state conference, at Essex Community College, outside Baltimore, had the most varied testimony of the five conferences I attended. Arriving late for the first session, I heard nine prepared statements and some informal interaction, as follows:

> A professional social worker spoke in defense of her life-style. She divorced her first husband and is living with a new man without benefit of ceremony. He is good to her and her children idolize him. She said that they considered themselves to be a family and are irked by "simple-minded" people who are threatened by new ways.

> A young educational coordinator at a local community college was generally concerned about education's neglect of the family dimension. She thinks education needs to spend more time preparing the young for careers as parents.

> A young man spoke for the gay/lesbian community. He reminded the group that gays come from families and maintain their family ties, and consider themselves to have normal affectional bonds. He spoke generally of the difficulties they have in contemporary society.

Some of the scheduled speakers had not arrived, so the chairpersons asked clarifying questions of the speakers. Two were directed at persons who had spoken before I arrived. A woman wanted employers to give persons like her the last half hour of work to relax, so she could get ready to face the demands of her family. A young man responded that his evangelical church would not accept the social worker's "live together" life-style.

> A young woman spoke about the "step-family." She said that terms like step-mother and step-father were still dirty words in our society, yet those labels apply

to a large proportion of the population. If you're a child and like your step-parent, you can't buy, for instance, a Happy Step-Father's Day card on father's day.

A woman described herself as an active member of the Maryland League of Women Voters. She ran through a rather lengthy list of government-supported services that benefit families; she stressed the importance of the role of the woman; she described the role of the League of Women Voters.

A man identified himself as being from the Islamic community of Columbia, Maryland. He said that marriage is required in his religion and that he was concerned about the eroding impact individualism and materialism were having on the family's cohesiveness and sense of moral responsibility.

A woman identified herself as a full-time wife, thank you, and mother of seven children. She resented the use of tax monies to support day care centers (without regard to need) and generally defended her life-style. She came down hard on women's groups who exclude housewife and mother from their list of acceptable careers.

A young professional, employed to advance family life, was concerned that we hear too much about the problems of families and too little about their strengths. He maintained that there are natural support systems that people live in daily and we must learn to reinforce these rather than create artificial, separate service systems.

A woman was concerned about adolescent pregnancy. She was nervous and drifted badly most of the time.

To fill in time, a chairperson asked the representative of the Islamic community whether his religion would accept the gay man over there or the life-style of the social worker over here. "No."

In a separate building a large lounge had been made available for interested persons to meet those who were running for the two elected delegate slots to the summer WHCF. The first two I talked with demonstrated the considerable differences among the candidates.

One woman was a Baltimore City teacher who resented using tax dollars to support abortions. She claimed to be active in many civic organizations in the state and had done much in the past for pure water.

Another woman was a Baltimore City teacher who favored the extended family. She was worried about society's mental set that considers the nuclear family to be the preferred type and, thus, considers all others to be deviants of that type. She would like the government to study how much money it saves because of the nation's extended families. Does she have an idea of how the government can support the extended family? Yes, with tax credits. Has she ever put her thoughts on paper? Yes, and she showed me a paper entitled "The Black Extended Family." Would she send me a copy? Yes, she would.

Outside the building, various booths and individuals handed out brochures with biographical sketches of their candidates. Two of the brochures are particularly interesting because they provide sketches of *two* candidates, apparently in the hope that the tandem would capture both available delegate slots. The sketches in the first brochure:

Senator Francis Kelly. Sen. Kelly is currently serving in the Maryland legislature representing the 5th District (portions of Baltimore, Carroll, and Harford Counties). Sen. Kelly has been a strong defender of the pro-life position on abortion funding on the Senate floor. He is married, has five children, and is self-employed as an insurance executive with Kelly and Assoc. Some of his awards and community involvement include: serving on the Parish Council of St. Joseph's Catholic Church, member of the Board of Directors of Quarter-Way Houses, Inc., member of the Maryland State Advisory Board on Foster Care, recipient of the Man of the Year Award 1974 presented by the Timonium-Cockeysville Jaycees, coach and manager in the Cockeysville-Springlake Recreation Council.

Jim Duncan. Jim is a member of the Maryland Bar and President of Duncan-Byrnes Inc., an investment real estate firm. Jim received a B.A. degree from Wheaton College at Wheaton, Ill., as well as secondary education certification from the state of Illinois. Jim and his wife, Jeanie, have a 2-year-old son and reside in Timonium. They are members of the Timonium Presbyterian Church, where they have been active as sponsors of the young people's group. Jim is concerned that evangelical Christians actively stand against the trends of secular humanism and government encouragement of these trends particularly as they devalue the dignity of human life and assault the integrity of the traditional family.

The second brochure was more elaborate, was printed on glossy paper, and contained photographs of the two candidates. The biographical sketches:

Dale Elliman Balfour. Dale Balfour, a resident of Baltimore County, has been involved in community activities for many years. She is presently a member of the Board of Directors of the First Step Multi-Service Youth Center, a member of the Baltimore County Planning Board, an elected member of the Platform Advisory Committee of the Democratic National Committee, and the President of the Action Policies Political Club. Mrs. Balfour's past volunteer activities include: serving as President of the Maryland League of Women Voters, teaching Sunday School, and working with retarded children at Kernan Hospital. She is married and the mother of two teenage children.

John Richard Bryant. Reverend John Bryant, the Pastor of Bethel A.M.E. Church, is married, the father of two children, and a man dedicated to community involvement. He is currently working to develop a full-service Jobs Program and a prison ministry through his church. Reverend Bryant has preached on four continents and has lectured at colleges and universities all over the country. His board memberships include: Freedom House, the governing Board of the National Council of Churches, and the Board of Regents of Morgan State University. He has won numerous honors and awards for his humanitarian efforts. He has been a teacher in the U.S. Peace Corps and at Harvard and Boston Universities.

The other state conferences at Penn State University, Wesley College in Delaware, and in a library on Maryland's Eastern Shore were similar in most respects to the two described above. In all cases the sincerity of the participants was intense; the points of view, varied; the expectations, hopeful; and the backgrounds of the participants, diverse. The subgroup of the population that

seemed best represented was the female parent. Most of the males in atten-
dance seemed to be clergymen, teachers, or employees of the social welfare
service system. Except for the Delaware hearing, children were in limited
supply and, except for the Penn State hearing, the aged were in limited
numbers. Blacks seemed underrepresented at three of the five hearings.

The candidates to represent the Eastern Shore of Maryland at the WHCF
were few enough in number to do a quick analysis of the posted biographical
sketches. Of the 17 candidates, 13 were female, 17 were white, and all but
one had a B.A. or more. The ages ranged from 28 to 53, with 12 in their
thirties. Extrapolating from this limited exposure at five state conferences
yielded the feeling that interest nationwide in the family and public policy was
awesome in scope and in intensity.

Nationwide, the issues resulting from the state conferences reflected the
diversity of the participants. South Dakota's top ten issues were:

1. Tax structure unfair to people choosing homemaking as a career.
2. Changes in social service programs to stop undermining the family unit
   and encourage families to live in the same household and become more
   self-reliant.
3. Making employment policies more supportive of working parents.
4. The need for parenthood education for youth.
5. The problem of relocation of the elderly, including loss of self-esteem,
   respect, and independence; and the parallel problems of quality nursing
   home care and insufficient family support.
6. Implementation of parental responsibility to the school system.
7. The need for adults to receive parenthood education, marriage enrichment, and communication skills training.
8. Assisting the handicapped in finding gainful employment.
9. Encouraging families to spend more quality time together.
10. The need to provide resources for displaced homemakers.

By the time the first of the WHCFs was held in Baltimore in June, 1980,
most of the states had submitted complete or partial reports on the principal
issues raised by their participants and recommendations derived from them.
Some of the major recommendations:

Thirty-five states made recommendations on government and families, including 19 that addressed the need for policies, legislation, and regulations to
be *supportive of families*.

Thirty-one states made recommendations that addressed economic pressures
and their effects on families. Of those, 22 states addressed *inflation* and
its effects on families.

Twenty-three states made recommendations in the area of *unemployment* and
job opportunities.

Twenty-six states made recommendations in support of *flex-time* policies.
Nineteen states recommended *elimination of the marriage tax penalty.*
Nineteen states called for *tax incentives* such as tax credits to care for an
    elderly or handicapped family member or a dependent child.
Twelve states recommended changes in the Social Security System to recog-
    nize the economic contributions of *homemakers* and to treat homemakers
    more equitably.
Thirty-two states made recommendations that addressed issues related to edu-
    cation, including 17 that addressed the *responsiveness of public educa-
    tion* to families.
Twenty-nine states made recommendations that addressed *family violence,*
    including 17 that addressed the availability of family violence programs
    and community services.

For the most part, the states had done a superb job of providing an open
forum for their citizens and selecting delegates to the national WHCF.

Press Coverage

Not all had gone smoothly and without controversy from the creation of the
WHCF to the summer national conventions, and the media, especially the
newspapers, took notice. Lynn Langway, Lucy Howard, and Donna Foote
wrote the most comprehensive report on the WHCF's problems in *Newsweek*
(January 28, 1980). They cited the Administration's initial choice of executive director and chairperson of the WHCF, and the response to it: "When the
Administration tapped a black, divorced mother of three—Health, Education
and Welfare official Patsy Fleming—as executive director, some outraged
Roman Catholics demanded a male co-director from an 'intact family.' Fleming resigned, and the chairperson, Wilbur Cohen, soon followed, citing ill
health." They saw the divergent views that were emerging as "the biggest
political battleground between conservatives and liberals since the National
Women's Conference in Houston in 1977."

> The factions basically divide over what they consider the proper role of govern-
> ment in family life. The conservatives, a well-organized cadre of about 150
> anti-abortion, anti-ERA groups who call themselves "Pro-Family," believe
> the Federal government shouldn't even be discussing family matters in the
> first place. A looser network of moderate-to-liberal groups, ranging from the
> American Home Economics Association to the National Gay Task Force, gener-
> ally favors some Federal funding to meet day-care and other family needs.

Langway, Howard, and Foote focused more on the efforts of the conservatives. "The conservatives quickly mobilized for the first (state) conventions
in Virginia and Oklahoma last fall and swept the elected slates." "Behind this
effort stand such experienced organizers as Phyllis Schlafly of Stop-ERA and
Eagle Forum, and Connaught Marshner, chairman of the Pro-Family Coali-

tion. Both object to the conference, but they say they want to register their dissent. The conservatives, for example, want 'families' defined as 'persons who are related by blood, marriage or adoption.' "

Edith Pendleton reported in the *Nashville Banner* (3/1/80): "During the first three hours of the conference's forums divorce, homosexuality, violence on television, sex education in public schools, welfare and prayer came up, rose to debate, then fell into the boiling pot of controversy left hanging until discussions resumed today."

Eric Nalder of the *Seattle Post-Intelligencer* (3/2/80) cited activities outside the conference center as reflecting the debates inside. "Picket signs outside the Seattle conference at Sealth High School foretold of controversy. 'Mormons have no rights to my rights,' said one. Others proclaimed opposition to abortion. Another sign expressed a cynical view of the intention of the conference to get grassroots opinions on problems facing the family."

Although all 50 states and seven territories were invited to appoint state coordinators and although all did initially, two states—Indiana and Alabama—pulled out of the process, with the latter receiving more attention. Kate Harris of the *Birmingham News* (2/14/80) reported that "Governor Fob James' wife, Bobbie, who ordinarily prefers to remain out of the limelight, is now at the center of a squabble over her and her husband's reluctance to send delegates from the state to the controversial White House Conference on Families." In a letter sent to NAC Chairperson Tucker, Mrs. James said that "the conference does not define 'what is a family' and leaves to chance that traditional Judeo-Christian family values would prevail."

Still, an analysis of a rather impressive accumulation of press clippings reveals a preoccupation with the aggressive stances of the conservatives, particularly Phyllis Schlafly and Connaught Marshner. Nadine Brozan of the *New York Times* (1/7/80) said: "What the 'pro-family' forces would most like to see is dissolution of the conference. Phyllis Schlafly said, the other day, 'Pro-family groups don't think the Federal Government has the competence to deal with the family: it aggravates problems rather than solves them.' " On the eve of the first WHCF in Baltimore, Sandy Banisky of the *Baltimore Sun* (6/1/80) reported: "Meanwhile, even as some pro-family groups plan to attend Thursday's session of the White House conference, they are planning a 'counter conference,' the American Family Forum, at Washington's Shoreham Hotel. The announced dates are June 29 to July 2. 'It's for people who want to hear the other side,' said National Pro-Family Coalition's Connaught Marshner, who calls the conference 'a farce.' "

Not all of the press coverage of the controversy was neutral. An editorial in the *Washington Post* (5/31/80) put it this way: "The very scheduling of this conference—to be held in successive sessions in several cities—has occasioned a remarkable amount of hassling and bad will among various single-interest groups. They have approached it as a forum in which either to press their views or to defend them against assault from other quarters. But despite the uproar by the 'pro-life' lobby, the abortion rights lobby, the gay rights lobby, the pro-family lobby and all the rest, the conference holds serious promise.'' David Gerke wrote more pointedly to the *New Mexican* after attending two state conferences in his state: ''The Los Alamos meeting was dominated by roots who heaped fertilizer on their own viewpoints while giving all other roots a liberal dose of herbicide.'' ''The feelings produced by these two gatherings are more appropriate to a buffalo stampede than they are to an enlightened, growing experience.''

The press corps waited eagerly for the Baltimore WHCF.

National Organization Activities and Issue Work Groups

For the general purpose of capacity building, the WHCF staff undertook an ambitious agenda of endeavors, not the least of which was the National Research Forum on Family Issues, held in the U.S. House of Representatives on April 10-11, 1980. Panels of experts read and reacted to papers on the following 24 topics:

Family Strengths and Supports
Diversity of Families (Racial and Ethnic Diversity)
Diversity of Families (Structurally Diverse Families)
The Changing Realities of Family Life
   a. A Historical Perspective
   b. Changes in Economic Aspects of Family Life
The Impact of Discrimination (Sex and Family Structure)
The Impact of Discrimination (Race, Ethnicity, Religion, Age, Sex, and
    Socioeconomic Status)
Families with Children
The Impact (of Public and Private Institutional Policies)—Education
The Impact—How Do We Measure It
The Impact—Families and the Workplace
The Impact—Income Maintenance and Financial Assistance to Families
The Impact—Social Services: Child Welfare Services
Families and the Aging
Families with Handicapping Conditions
The Impact—Housing
The Impact—Media
The Impact—Health
The Impact—Child Care
Religion and Family Life
The Impact—Judicial System: Alternative Ways of Settling Family
    Disputes/Patterns in Family Law
The Impact of Incarceration on Families

Special Family Conditions—Family Violence
Special Family Conditions—Adolescent Pregnancy
Special Family Conditions—Substance Abuse

Contacts with national organizations ranged from information sharing to the production of major reports, two of which were a major compendium of data by the Bureau of the Census, entitled *American Families and Living Together,* and a report on a study of 46,817 respondents by *Better Homes and Gardens,* entitled *Is Government Helping or Hurting American Families?*

Continuous input was provided by the Coalition for the White House Conference on Families. This coalition of 52 organizations had formed voluntarily to support the WHCF and contained an unlikely assortment of members, for example:

Aid Association for Lutherans
American College of Nurse Midwives
American Home Economics Association
American Red Cross
B'nai B'rith Women
Family Service Association of America
National Conference of Catholic Charities
National Gay Task Force
Planned Parenthood—World Population

Miscellaneous Independent Activities

Not all family policy initiatives in this period were started by the WHCF, but many were related to it in one way or another. The following is a sampling of such independent activities from the end of the state WHCF activities in March, 1980, to the Baltimore WHCF in June.

Revival of Fundamental Religion   James Mann wrote in the April 7, 1980, issue of *U.S. News and World Report* that conservative religion is on the "offensive." He states that most U.S. church members still adhere to relatively liberal versions of Protestantism and Catholicism, but defections over the past 15 years have reduced membership by as much as 25%.

At the same time, Mann states, conservative religious groups such as Mormons, Southern Baptists, and Seventh-Day Adventists have been growing by rates as high as 4% per year, which accounts for about 20% of the U.S. population.

Political activism is a core ingredient of the conservative religious groups. According to Mann, "Nationally syndicated preachers such as Pat Robertson, Jerry Falwell and James Robison have been urging viewers to vote a strongly conservative line on such issues as abortion, welfare, pornography, big government, Communism and defense." Voting for delegates to the WHCF is seen as one of the successes of their political activism, Mann stated.

The Division of Black Affairs, HHS   From April 30 through May 2, 1980, a symposium was held in the nation's capitol entitled "Policy and Program Issues Related to Child and Family Services to Black Americans." The symposium was planned under contract from the Division of Black American Affairs, HHS. The focus was on services rather than families or individuals, especially foster care and adoption, day care, child abuse and neglect, adolescent pregnancy, Title XX, and miscellaneous others. No distinction was made between the needs of individuals and the needs of families.

In contrast to the WHCF, there was no controversy here. A governmental role relative to black families seemed self-evidently appropriate and the focus of the discussions was on how to improve that role, on how to make it more sensitive to and more responsive to the needs of black families.

A Senate Speech   On May 9, 1980, Senator Gordon J. Humphrey of New Hampshire attacked the White House Conference on Families' process in a blistering speech in the U.S. Senate (27 pages in the Congressional Record, Vol. 126, No. 75). Accepting the concerns of the pro-family movement and citing the negative press of the WHCF, he concluded as follows (excerpts):

> Growing numbers of Americans are outraged by the series of Carter White House projects on topics related to the American family. Taxpayers in large numbers have written me to ask why they should be forced to provide a platform for the social service bureaucrats and assorted counterculture zealots. I am asked why taxes pressed from the flesh of our Nation's families should be put at the disposal of Bella Abzug and her successors who have run the bizarre series of White House "commissions" relating to the family.

> The track record is plain for all to see. The aim of those who have control of these White House projects has been to increase Government involvement in family matters which traditionally have been outside the scope of Government. Gay rights, kiddie rights, abortion on demand, Government child care centers, and ever larger numbers of Government bureaucrats purportedly "helping" people by taxing away the resources of families: these are all part of the pattern.

> As to the upcoming White House Conference on Families, there is no need for it. The problems and burdens of the American family are painfully obvious: searing inflation, punitive taxation, breath-taking interest rates, declining quality of public education, and the encouragement of decadence by governmental institutions. The last thing the American family needs now is more meddling from President Carter and his legion of social engineers. Let the government attend to getting its own house in order, so that families can have some chance of economic survival. Most American families ask no more and want no more.

A HHS Conference   On May 19 and 20, 1980, there was a conference in Washington entitled "Research on Children and Adolescents in the Family Context," sponsored jointly by the (federal) Interagency Panel on Early Childhood Research and Development and the (federal) Interagency Panel for Research and Development on Adolescence. This annual conference had not before had a family context; the organizers made this change because it was "timely."

Dr. Rueben Hill's presentation at the conference was cited liberally in Chapter 1 (see "Professional/Scientific Interest in the Family").

A Special Issue of the Conservative Digest   The entire May/June issue of the *Conservative Digest,* featuring Senator Paul Laxalt on the cover, was devoted to the pro-family movement. The pro-family movement was described as a coalition of individuals and groups, many of which are relatively new to the public scene, but share a common conservative ideology and a common commitment to several issues. Photographs and capsule resumés were given for 62 of its leaders, grouped into eight sets.

1. Thirteen members of Congress were identified, including Jesse Helms (R-N.C.) and Paul Laxalt (R-Nev.) from the Senate, and Henry Hyde (R-Ill.) and Larry McDonald (D-Ga.) from the House.
2. Eight persons were identified as constituting the "Washington Connection," including Bob Baldwin (Citizens for Educational Freedom) and Connie Marshner (Family Policy Division of the Free Congress).
3. Ten persons were listed under "Pro-Family Organizations," including Father Virgil Blum (Catholic League for Religious and Civil Rights) and Phyllis Schlafly (Eagle Forum).
4. Seventeen "Evangelicals" were listed, including Jerry Falwell (The Moral Majority), Adrian Rogers (Southern Baptist Convention), and Pat Robertson (host of "The 700 Club").
5. Eight leaders of the pro-life movement were listed, including Paul Brown (Life Amendment Political Action Committee) and Peter Gemma (National Pro-Life Political Action Committee).
6-8. Two persons were listed under each of the categories of Education, Anti-Pornography, and Anti-Homosexuals, the most widely known of which was Anita Bryant.

It was not apparent in the text how strongly each of the 62 leaders identified himself and herself with the "Pro-Family Movement," nor was it clear how closely any two of the leaders work together, nor was it clear how large a constituency was represented by the leaders. It did seem, however, that the term "Pro-Family" was becoming a broadly accepted umbrella term for diverse Christian political activists who have a common conservative ideology and some well-defined issues to rally around. In a separate interview, Paul Weyrich, founder of the Committee for the Survival of a Free Congress, maintained that family issues will dominate the 1980s and the conservatives, growing larger in number daily and more politically astute as well, will take the initiative and dominate.

A leading role in this initiative was accorded to Senator Laxalt, who had introduced the Family Protection Act (S. 1808, as amended, and H.R. 6028, as amended) to the Senate Finance Committee in the fall of 1979. In due time, that committee referred it for Executive comment, a delaying tactic that would bury the bill until after the fall elections. There are five titles in the act, which contain a grand total of 38 provisions. A sampling:

Title I—Education (16 provisions)
  1. Federal education money is denied states that do not allow prayer in public buildings.
  12. A Family Savings for Education Plan is established: Parents may deposit up to $2,500, tax-exempt, per year, to save for their children's education.

Title II—Welfare (5 provisions)
  18. A tax exemption of $1,000 is allowed a household which includes a dependent person age 65 or over.
  20. A corporation may deduct from taxes its contributions to a joint employee-employer day care facility.

Title III—First Amendment Guarantees (2 provisions)
  23. Rights of Families. Parental rights over the religious and moral upbringing of their children are reinforced.

Title IV—Taxation (5 provisions)
  24. Contributions by an employed person to a savings account for his nonworking spouse are tax deductible, up to $1,500 per year.
  25. The current "marriage tax," which penalizes married couples with two incomes, is eliminated.

Title V—Domestic Relations (10 provisions)
  32. Parents must be informed when an unmarried minor receives contraceptive appliances or abortion-related services from a federally supported organization.
  38. Discrimination against declared homosexuals may not be considered an "unlawful employment practice."

A Gallup Poll In March of 1980 George Gallup, Jr. probed the opinions of 1592 U.S. adults on the family, releasing the results to the press just before the Baltimore WHCF. Eight out of 10 responded that the family was the most important element in their lives, but 45% felt that family life has worsened over the past 15 years and 37% were disquieted about the future.

Asked to identify the most harmful influences on family life, 60% listed drug abuse and 59% identified alcohol abuse. Asked to identify the most important problems facing families, 81% named the high cost of living and 53% listed energy costs. Toward the bottom of the list were adequate health care, child care, education, and conflict between job and family responsibilities. To help them cope with the interdependence of job and family responsibilities, the respondents wanted flexible work hours, sick leave if a family member is ill, and a four-day work week.

The $59,000 survey was conducted with private funds, but was coordinated with WHCF activities.

IMPLEMENTATION: THE SUMMER CONFERENCES

General Procedure

Each of the conferences was to have about 650 official delegates. The delegate body would break down into four "Broad Topic Groups," and from there down to 20 "Small Workshop Groups." Each of the small groups would entertain candidate policy recommendations (maximum of 100 words), selecting the three highest for voting first in the Broad Topic Groups and then in the total delegate body. Thus, a maximum of 60 policy recommendations would be voted on by the delegate assembly. The Broad Topic Groups and the Small Workshop Groups were as follows:

Broad Topic Groups	Small Workshop Groups
A. Families and Economic Well-Being	1. Economic Pressures
	2. Family and Work
	3. Tax Policies
	4. Income Security for Families
	5. Status of Homemakers
B. Families: Challenges and Responsibilities	6. Preparation for Marriage and Family Life
	7. Specific Supports and Families
	8. Parents and Children
	9. Family Violence
	10. Substance Abuse
	11. Aging and Families
C. Families and Human Needs	12. Education
	13. Health
	14. Housing
	15. Child Care
	16. Handicapping Conditions
D. Families and Major Institutions	17. Government
	18. Media
	19. Community Institutions
	20. Law and the Judicial System

The Baltimore Conference

The delegate body seemed generally happy with the 60 recommendations. For each of them, the delegates voted on a four-point scale of strongly agree/moderately agree/moderately disagree/strongly disagree, and the 35,037 total ballots cast (an average of 584 per recommendation) are distributed on the scale as follows:

	No.	%
Strongly agree	22,422	64.0%
Moderately agree	6,744	19.2%
Moderately disagree	2,565	7.3%
Strongly disagree	3,306	9.4%
	35,037	99.9%

To rank the 60 recommendations, the "strongly agree" and "moderately agree" ballots were combined and divided by the number of ballots cast per recommendation to yield a "percentage favorable" score for each recommendation. The results:

% favorable	No. of recommendations
90% or higher	26
80% to 89.9%	19
70% to 79.9%	7
60% to 69.9%	1
50% to 59.9%	4
less than 50%	3
	60

The range of percentage favorable scores was from 37.5% to 97.5%.

Although the beneficiaries of the recommendations were somewhat predetermined by the subjects of the 20 workshop groups, the segments of society that were targeted for implementing them were more within the control of the workshop delegates. The distribution of the targeted implementors is as follows:

Principal targeted implementors	No. of recommendations
Federal government	11
Other government	3
Government at all levels	20
Government and private sector	16
Private sector	1
Unspecified	5
Other	4
	60

Clearly the government is the principal targeted implementor. Many of the recommendations distinguished between the executive and legislative branches of government, and the recommendations of workshop No. 20 focused specifically on the judicial system.

Virtually all of the recommendations seem to require additional funding of existing programs for expansion or modifications, and some require additional legislative authority.

The recommendations at the extremes of the ranking deserve some attention here, as do the recommendations that polarized the delegates the most. The top four recommendations in percentage of favorable votes were as follows. From the workshop group, Substance Abuse, in the topic group, Families: Challenges and Responsibilities; 97.5% in favor:

As substance abuse, including alcohol, causes many severe family problems, preventive programs should include:

a. Schools, K-12, and agencies should provide educational and vocational preventive studies concerning dangers of alcohol, drug abuse, abuse of prescription drugs, and the necessity of positive parental example.

b. Media should avoid showing drugs as a cure-all, promote public awareness of constructive alternatives, and must provide equal time to counteract alcohol commercials.

c. There should be a movement toward parental meetings, both with and without children, to educate them regarding prevention.

d. Medical professionals should undergo extensive training on drug abuse, especially prescription drugs and alcohol.

From the workshop group, Handicapping Conditions, in the topic group, Families and Human Needs; 97.0% in favor:

Educate the public and private sectors to the value of handicapped persons in our society to achieve total integration.

a. education of employers and employees to capabilities and needs of handicapped persons within the work force;

b. appropriate training of handicapped persons for career, home and life skills;

c. organizations and institutions build into their professional school curricula standards for accreditation, in-service training, the appropriate educational information and requirements to create a responsive service delivery system;

d. use of handicapped persons to promote national media campaign to educate the public; and

e. secondary educational curricula include practical work with handicapped persons.

From the workshop group, Family and Work, in the topic group, Families and Economic Well-Being; 96.4% in favor:

Business, labor and government should encourage and implement employment opportunities and personnel policies that enable persons to hold jobs while maintaining a strong family life. Family-oriented policies can result in reduced absenteeism, greater productivity and decreased stress. Toward such desirable ends there is need for creative development of such work arrangements as flextime, flexible leave policies for both sexes, job sharing programs, dependent care options and part-time jobs with pro-rated pay and benefits. Additionally, employers should recognize the possible adverse effects of relocation on families so that they may provide support and options.

From the workshop group, Aging and Families, in the topic group, Families: Challenges and Responsibilities; 96.3% in favor:

To encourage home care support alternatives to institutionalization and promote choice for families and the elderly, we recommend:

   a. appropriate changes in Medicaid/Medicare policies;
   b. tax benefits to cover costs incurred for homemaker services, day care, night
      care, transportation, and appropriate home improvements;
   c. local development of services by the public or private sectors such as tele-
      phone reassurances, meals on wheels, friendly visiting, companionship,
      dial-a-ride and respite care;
   d. funding services to help elderly individuals maintain their own homes.

These top-ranked recommendations are nonoverlapping—substance
abuse, handicapped persons, family-oriented personnel policies, and benefits
for the elderly. Furthermore, whereas 34 of the 60 recommendations are
targeted to government, all four of those are targeted both to the public and
private sector.

   That substance abuse was top-ranked is surprising. A large proportion of
the delegate body was young adults who had grown up amidst permissive
values about drugs. Perhaps the delegate election/appointment process
selected out those who do not consider some drugs to be socially acceptable
commodities. The other three top-ranked recommendations seemed compassionate and noncontroversial.

   The least favored recommendation came from the workshop group,
Media, in the topic group, Families and Major Institutions; 37.5% in favor:

   All media must present views in a balanced manner on all issues of concern.
   American families rest on a foundation of diversity. Such diversity is sorely
   lacking in the models provided by the mass media both in advertising and in the
   content of entertainment fare, much of which ridicules strong family relations
   and provides negative roles for children and other family members. Stereotyped
   portrayals of women and minorities are particularly destructive and dangerous.

Interestingly, this least-favored recommendation also does not target government for implementation.

   The other two recommendations that received less than 50% affirmative
votes were concerned with the federal government's assuming 100% funding
responsibility for ensuring a minimum living standard for all and for providing
tax incentives to couples to participate in experiential programs regarding
marriage responsibility.

   Two recommendations polarized the group more than any others. One
came from the workshop group, Government, in the topic group, Families and
Major Institutions. The polarity is apparent from the distribution of the 583
ballots cast: 250 (strongly agree), 42 (moderately agree), 58 (moderately
disagree), and 233 (strongly disagree); 50.1% favored the recommendation
and 83% of the ballots were "strongly" in one direction or the other:

   We support policies which preserve and protect basic legal and human rights of
   all family members. To guarantee these rights we support:

   a. Ratification of the ERA.
   b. Elimination of discrimination and encouragement of respect for differences
      based on sex, race, ethnic origin, creed, socio-economic status, age, dis-
      ability, diversity of family type and size, sexual preference or biological ties.

c. Protection against violent and abusive action.
d. Right to open, accessible, accountable, and responsive government at all levels.
e. Right to decide whether or not to bear a child including access to the full range of family planning services, abortion, and maternal and infant care.

The other polarizing recommendation came from the workshop group, Health, in the topic group, Families and Human Needs. Of the 585 ballots cast, 96.5% were in the "strongly" categories and 65.5% overall favored the recommendation.

America was founded on deeply held principles of religious freedom, liberty and pluralism.
The decision whether to have a child is a personal decision of conscience for each woman in consultation with a doctor.
Government restrictions would endanger the health and well-being of the woman and family.
Therefore, the full range of family planning services including pre- and post-natal care and safe, legal abortion must be available to all who freely make this decision.
Regarding abortion and all reproductive services, neither the WHCF nor the government should pass any proposal that should be mandatory for parent or child.

Identifying dominant themes at a conference such as this is highly subjective and is based more on personal observation than on reading the recommendations. Clearly the dominant theme was affirmative action for the family, and an increased, more efficient role for government was a not too distant second. Clearly the deepest feelings surrounded the abortion issue. Not so clear was the concern about pluralism, because it is not clear what that means to people—homosexuality? open marriages? serial monogamy? female-headed households? unions without ceremony? It is difficult to say. There did appear to be a small, but strong, concern about the ever-expanding presence of government; this is the tip of the iceberg, since persons holding that view are probably not as likely to run for delegates from their states to such a conference as their more activist neighbors. Overall, however, the delegates seemed to work well together in spite of the pluralism of their backgrounds. Expectedly, the recommendations cover the waterfront and, expectedly, they are general, but their composition is fascinating because it represents what people in the eastern states were willing to work to say. Interestingly, expectations of open conflict and controversy were not fulfilled. Several dozen conservatives walked out, but their absence went largely unnoticed except by some members of the press.

The Minneapolis and Los Angeles Conferences

The Minneapolis and Los Angeles conferences differed only slightly from the Baltimore conference. The same process of generating recommendations was used, and most of them received over 50% favorable votes.

Conservative blocs again expressed their displeasure with the conduct of the conference and the liberal recommendations that emanated from some workshop groups. About 150 conservatives walked out of the Minneapolis conference, but returned for most of the balloting. In Los Angeles there was some ballot-tearing, but no significant walkout. The incendiary issues again proved to be abortion, variant family life-styles, and the Equal Rights Amendment.

The degree of polarization of delegates was greatest at the Minneapolis conference. In Baltimore, 16.7% of the ballots on the recommendations had been negative and 18.5% in Los Angeles, but 27.7% of the Minneapolis votes were negative.

Since the same format of 20 preselected small workshop groups was used in all three conferences, the recommendations from them overlapped considerably. It was the job of the National Task Force to integrate the three sets of recommendations, and the results of their efforts are discussed in the next chapter. (The recommendations from the Baltimore conference are presented *in toto* in the Appendix at this end of this book.)

Although press coverage of the Minneapolis and Los Angeles conferences was less voluminous than in Baltimore, it tended to be positive in tone, even in its coverage of the controversies. Several columns dwelled at length on the productive feelings many representatives expressed. Two of the three major TV networks provided specials on the WHCF process.

Miscellaneous Independent Activities

Throughout the summer of 1980, there continued to be a variety of independent activities that were in some way related to the conduct of the WHCF.

An Article in **America**   In the June 14, 1980, issue of *America,* Bishop J. Francis Stafford wrote of his early experiences on the WHCF's National Advisory Committee, especially his misgivings about "pluralism." His main message, however, dealt with priorities. In his opinion, reduction of joblessness and poverty is the *sine qua non* of American public policy for families. His article develops that stance and reflects a rather liberal view of the role of government.

A Syndicated Columnist Speaks Out   In his June 14, 1980, column, James J. Kilpatrick reported that there had been the "noisy" WHCF in Baltimore run by social activists. The other one was held in Washington, D.C., sponsored with private funds from the American Family Institute. "It was as one-sidely conservative as the Baltimore affair was one-sidely liberal. Participants were not concerned with getting government into family affairs; they were concerned with keeping government out."

Two of the principal speakers were Justice William Rehnquist of the Supreme Court and Paul Johnson of the American Enterprise Institute.

Actions by and against Catholic Groups   The Associated Press on June 28, 1980, reported on two events in the Catholic community. One was the decision that, although they would continue to support the WHCF, the U.S. Catholic Conference and the National Conference of Catholic Charities withdrew from the Coalition for the WHCF—an assemblage of organizations that had long supported the WHCF. The second report read:

> An antiabortion group yesterday filed suit against the bishops of all 170 Catholic dioceses in the United States, complaining they were guilty of "unwarranted harassment" against pro-life advocates who want to discuss abortion issues at churches.
> Robert Sassone, the attorney who filed the suit on behalf of Life Amendment Political Action Committee, Inc., said the suit seeks an injunction to stop the bishops from imposing a ban on "soliciting signatures or distributing handbills in a reasonable manner which does not interfere with the normal business or worship activities of each church on the sidewalks and parking lots . . . in each of the dioceses."

An Article in **The New Republic**   In the June 28, 1980, issue of *The New Republic,* Diane Ravitch offered a much quoted, blistering treatise on all that was wrong with the WHCF, ending with a general commentary on family public policy. Some excerpts:

> The desire to have a harmonious, consistent, coherent national family policy is understandable. We know that a health policy aims to make people healthy; we know that the object of a housing policy is to house people. But we cannot construct a family policy when we have neither a generally accepted understanding of what a family is nor of what such a policy should accomplish.
>
> To the extent that the agenda of family policy is directed to such clear-cut, but currently unfashionable issues as child welfare and maternal health, or to children's allowances and a guaranteed minimum income, then the possibility of devising a national consensus and a national policy exists. But if the agenda for formulating family policy continues to be a vehicle for the concerns of special issue groups, be they feminists, homosexuals, professional service providers, the new left, or the new right, then the issue will be mired in terminal political and ideological controversy.

The American Family Forum   The pro-family movement held its counter-conference, the American Family Forum, at Washington, D.C.'s Shoreham Hotel from June 30 to July 2, 1980—three days of sessions sponsored by the Free Congress Foundation for about 600 attendees. Senator Paul Laxalt, sponsor of the Family Protection Act, was a keynote speaker, being introduced as one of the six finalists for a vice-presidency with Ronald Reagan. He said he would not press for hearings on his bill until after the fall elections.

The following sessions were featured in the conference program:

First Day
   Children's Legal Rights: Problems and Prospects
   Religious Traditions and the Family
   The Family and the General Culture: Negative Impact of Public Policy
   Professionals vs. the Family
   National Economic Policy and the Family
   The Problem of Homosexuality vs. the Family
   The Family and Education: A Legal Perspective
   The Battle for the Mind
   Pornography
   Young + Old = Growth: Renewing Communication Within the Family
   How to Survive the War Against the Family
Second Day
   Focus on the Family
   Planned Parenthood and Teenage Sexuality
   Involving Church Women
   TV and the General Culture
   How to Improve Children's Textbooks
   School Can Wait
   Euthanasia: The Ultimate Strike Against the Family
   Impact of Religious Education on Character Development and the Family
   Politics of the Family
   American (Christian) Couples
   The Family in Soviet Society
   The Family: Key to Survival
Third Day
   Children's Lib Debate
   The Legal Status of the Family
   Home Grown Kids
   Sexual Suicide
   The Church: The Alternative to HEW
   Impact of IYC and the WHCF
   Virtue in the Family
   Cable TV and the Family
   Helping Your Children in School
   Homemakers as Policymakers

    With this conference the conservative bloc dispelled the notion that it was a single-issue movement.

    Legislation   In August, bills were introduced in the House and Senate to end the "marriage penalty" in the income tax system—an action unlikely to have occurred without the activities of the WHCF.

SUMMARY

(The implementation phase of the WHCF began in September of 1980 and is discussed in the next chapter. The summary here is limited to the "visible" part of the WHCF process as described above.)

The 1980 White House Conference on Families defies summarization. Just keeping track of its whirling-dervish agenda over a year was exhausting, and it will be quite some time before its full impact can be assessed.

Certainly one must conclude from the total experience that nationwide interest in family issues is intense. EVERYBODY participated—private citizens, the President and members of Congress, all sorts of professionals, advocacy groups, representatives of private industry, religious leaders, the media: friends and foes alike. Predictably, lack of total consensus yielded controversy. The most visible controversies were concerned with abortion, the Equal Rights Amendment, and variant family styles; less visible—perhaps less well articulated—were concerns about the efficiency of big government and the appropriateness of government's interest in the family.

The conservatives, under the banner of the pro-family movement, made their mark. They not only demonstrated an increasingly efficient propensity for political activism, but also reflected the view that healthy families—their real constituency—are best left alone by meddling government. They made the point very strongly that scientists and professional groups will not have a monopoly on influencing policy decision makers; persons and groups with solely a value base rather than a scientific base will increasingly press for favorable changes. And they have proclaimed the 1980s to be the decade of family issues.

Most of the representatives to the three summer conferences favored an increasingly attentive role for government. Although there was considerable concern about government's poor track record for efficiency, one Baltimore delegate summarized it thusly: "Is there a better alternative?" It is a highly subjective observation, but a reading of the 180 recommendations from the three summer conferences inclines one to sense the feeling that, although we need more government for families, we also need "better" government. For example, the following was the second highest ranked recommendation in Minneapolis:

> Public policies should help rather than hurt families. But when laws are enacted or implemented few if any organizations or individuals ask "how does this policy affect families?" As a result, many government policies are anti-family including the marriage penalty in the income tax, foster care policies and Medicare payments that favor institutional care over family care, and welfare laws that require the father to leave home for his family to receive assistance. We recommend, therefore, that laws and regulations be analyzed in terms of their impact on families.

It is difficult to assess the importance of the recommendations. All of them are general and will require the same type of careful policy analysis that would be needed even without the WHCF, if substantive action is to result. Furthermore, it is difficult to assess what the ranking by percentage of yes votes means. Are the highest ranked recommendations the most important or the least innocuous? Since no one pretends that the delegates to the three WHCFs constituted a statistically valid sample of the U.S. population, do the recommendations really represent the will of the people? Although much attention has been given to the ranked recommendations, it seems likely that they are the least important part of the WHCF output.

Perhaps the most important function of the WHCF was to provide a central forum for the swelling interest in family public policy. Many people from many different origins were ready to commit, and they did so— providing a timely sanction for a maturing policy issue. Unlike most other White House conferences in years past, which died quickly and amicably, it does not seem possible to stop the momentum generated by the 1980 WHCF. There will be spillover from the Catholic Decade of the Family. The conservative activists have promised legislative initiatives. Political leaders in both parties have committed themselves. The professional community has come of age. The citizenry wants progressive action and redress of grievances. In spite of specific areas of controversy, there is consensus that this topic is IMPOR-TANT, that the family has indelibly become a policy issue, that the family will become THE issue of the 1980s. Only time will tell how well this raw energy expresses itself in public policy.

Chapter 5

An Emerging Federal Effort

From the fall of 1979 to the Presidential elections in the fall of 1980, a series of developments constituted the first cautious steps toward a deliberate federal effort on behalf of families—an effort characterized more by its unprecedented explicitness than its probable effectiveness in the short run. The White House Conference on Families process was the most visible effort, but also one with a predetermined ending date.

THE OFFICE FOR FAMILIES

In an October 15, 1979, address to the National Conference of Catholic Charities in Kansas City, President Carter announced: "I am . . . announcing today that Health, Education and Welfare Secretary Patricia Harris is creating for the first time an office for families within HEW. I know you agree with me that this is long overdue. I want to make sure that this office is not only involved in the preparation for the [White House Conference on Families] and helping to make the conference a success, but after the conference work is completed, this office, a permanent entity within HEW, will be there as a focal point to carry out the recommendations of the conference itself." Thus was created the first official element in the bureaucracy to specialize in family policy and programs.

Shortly before the President's October 15 announcement, a decision memorandum circulated through HEW (now HHS), seeking decisions on the scope and location of the new Office for Families (OF). It was addressed to the Secretary of HEW from the Assistant Secretary for Human Development Services (HDS) in HEW. It cited prior correspondence in which a decision had been made to establish the OF in HDS with an initial staff of six and with the following functions:

1. Advocate on behalf of the family and coordinate program policy that impacts on family life.

2. Serve as a focus for the integration of policy relating to the family.
3. Assume limited relevant research analysis functions.

Relative to the scope of the new office's functions, three options were given: 1) have the Office perform its functions in relation to HDS programs only; 2) broaden the Office's functions to relate to all HHS programs; or 3) have the Office perform its functions on a government-wide basis. Relative to the issue of where to locate the Office within HDS, two options were given: 1) locate it within the Administration for Children, Youth and Families (one of the principal components of HDS) or 2) locate it within the Immediate Office of the Assistant Secretary for Human Development Services. The decision memorandum recommended placing the new OF in the Immediate Office of the HDS Assistant Secretary with an HHS-wide scope.

Although the final and full scope of OF's functions was not immediately and specifically decided, it was placed in HDS' Administration for Children, Youth and Families, which has been received with mixed reactions. On the favorable side, the mere creation of the Office for Families was received as a positive step forward; additionally, it seemed appropriate that the Administration on Children, Youth and Families should have such an office to complement its traditional child welfare orientation. On the negative side, some felt that it was placed too low in the hierarchy of the bureaucracy to deal effectively with issues that fall beyond the purview of the Administration on Children, Youth and Families—possibly issues in other sections of HDS, probably in the health sector of HHS, and nearly certainly in other federal departments such as Labor, Education, and Housing and Urban Development. And without question it could not effectively address major government-wide issues such as inflation. Finally, since it was created by executive fiat rather than Congressional mandate, OF could be disbanded by future administrations as easily as it had been created. Many persons therefore concluded that the creation of OF was a necessary and appropriate first step, but insufficient in itself for mounting and carrying out a broad-scale federal implementation plan.

The growth of OF has been less than promised. Six staffers in 1980 were to grow to 11 on October 1, 1980, the start of the new fiscal year. This growth was to coincide with the shift of the WHCF to its implementation stage in September through the spring of 1981, with OF assuming many implementation functions. However, one professional staffer carried most of the burden until October 1 and further growth was stalled by Congress's continuing resolution. (When Congress is unable to approve a new fiscal year's budget by the start of that year, it is customary to pass a "continuing resolution" that, in effect, continues the previous year's budget with no increases.) It was anticipated that the continuing resolution would delay growth at least until December, 1980.

At the time of this writing (November, 1980), therefore, the opinion of many is that OF has significant but limited potential, has an uncertain future, and has not grown at the very time it is needed most to maintain momentum created by the WHCF.

WHCF FINAL REPORT

In October of 1980 the WHCF released its final report, *Listening to America's Families: Action for the 80's,* which contained a description of its history, the final recommendations, and its implementation plan.

The recommendations of the Baltimore, Minneapolis, and Los Angeles conferences were combined and expressed in rank order. The final ordering is as follows (with percentage of yes votes by delegates in parentheses):

1. A call for family-oriented personnel policies—flexitime, leave policies, shared and part-time jobs, transfer policies. (92.7%)
2. New efforts to prevent alcohol and drug abuse—education and media initiatives. (92.7%)
3. Major changes in the tax code to eliminate the marriage tax penalty, revise inheritance taxes, and recognize homemakers. (92.1%)
4. Tax policies to encourage home care of aging and handicapped persons. (92.0%)
5. Greater assistance to families with a handicapped member—tax credits, financial help, etc. (91%)
6. A call for systematic analysis of all laws, regulations, and rules for their impact on families. (90.4%)
7. Efforts to increase public awareness and sensitivity toward persons with handicapping conditions. (90.1%)
8. Government efforts to assist handicapped persons—enforce existing laws, etc. (89.8%)
9. Encourage independence and home care for aging persons—tax incentives, housing programs. (89%)
10. More equitable economic treatment of full-time homemakers—Social Security changes, programs for displaced homemakers. (87.4%)
11. Reform of Social Security—eliminate biases against families, marriage, homemakers. (84.9%)
12. Increased pressure on media to curb excess violence, sex, stereotypes. (83.4%)
13. Increased efforts to combat employment discrimination. (83%)
14. Support for family violence prevention efforts services. (82%)
15. Involvement of families in improved family support services and self-help efforts. (81.5%)

16. Support for full employment—implement Humphrey-Hawkins Act, job creation efforts. (81.4%)
17. Development of coherent energy and inflation policy. (79.4%)
18. Promote and support a variety of child care choices—home, community, and center based care and parental choice. (79%)
19. Improved tax incentives for family housing. (78.3%)
20. Increased efforts to prevent and deal with adolescent pregnancy. (77.9%)

As stated earlier, there are few surprises in this list of recommendations, with the exception of the highest-ranked recommendation dealing with family-sensitive personnel policies such as flexitime. It is not clear whether that recommendation is highest ranked because it was viewed as most important or because it was viewed as a harmless, generally acceptable idea.

On October 22, President Carter released a three-page initial reaction to the report. It stated satisfaction with the work done by the WHCF and promised implementation, specifying seven initial steps.

1. It cited the assembly on that day of executives in the nation's largest firms to share findings on the need for family-sensitive personnel policies.
2. It promised efforts to repeal the "marriage tax penalty."
3. It referred to the creation of the Office for Families.
4. It alluded to an impending directive to all federal agencies "to undertake a thorough analysis of their policies and programs in light of the recommendations contained in the final report of the White House Conference on Families, and to develop detailed plans for implementing Conference proposals."
5. It stated that the Domestic Policy Staff would "make Conference recommendations an invariable criterion for the evaluation of policies and programs."
6. It promised to continue working with the National Advisory Committee of the WHCF.
7. It pledged a continuing working relationship with the private sector that serves American families.

Finally, the Presidential report stated that these seven steps were only the beginning of a long-term effort designed to have a positive impact on families.

The WHCF report outlined its six-month implementation plan, which began in September of 1980. The principal elements of the plan included: 1) communication of conference results, 2) continuing analysis of conference recommendations, 3) advocacy with key constituencies (e.g., academic institutions, business and labor institutions, religious groups), and 4) establishing vehicles for on-going implementation. Considerable attention was given to the role of the states in implementation; about 40 states had maintained coordinators who would undertake various implementation activities. However, most long-lasting benefits were seen as residing in initiatives undertaken by the legislative branches of the federal government.

It is difficult to assess the importance of the WHCF report or its potential impact. Certainly it is a comprehensive, interesting, attractive report, but it is by itself just a start. The unknown variables are how effective the WHCF staff will be during its implementation phase through the spring of 1981 and whether anyone or anything will emerge to replace the WHCF as a focal point of activity and coordination. Future leadership is one large question mark.

Perhaps the greatest obstacle to implementing the recommendations of the WHCF will be the indifference of the legion bureaucrats who must be involved in transferring the recommendations to the "policy machine" and who view White House conferences as homogeneously ineffective. The track record of previous White House conferences is notoriously poor. They generate, according to the average bureaucrat I have talked with, a great deal of hoopla and produce wild assortments of recommendations that add up to little more than "wish lists." It simply isn't a wise use of time, they maintain, to get too involved with a White House conference because, once the noise is over, things get back to "normal" quickly. The WHCF staff has been well aware of this attitude and intends to be the exception to the rule of the typical White House conference, but only time and a sound evaluation will determine the success or failure of their efforts.

THE 1980 CAMPAIGN

The country has been generally shifting toward a conservative view of government. The strong showing of the conservatives in the WHCF process was repeated even more forcefully in the 1980 Presidential campaign. In the primaries, moderate President Carter defeated the more liberal Ted Kennedy and conservative Reagan defeated the more liberal George Bush. Uncharacteristically, Republican challenger John Anderson was the most liberal candidate. The platforms of the three candidates were interesting and somewhat perplexing.

The Republican platform, read into the Congressional Record by Senator Howard Baker (Tenn.), was a lengthy document of 44 pages, each page having two columns of fine print. Three of the 95 topics were specifically addressed to the family (Strong Families, the Family Economy, and Family Protection), and the following paragraph was placed midway in the introductory statement of philosophy:

> This platform addresses many concerns of our Party. We seek to restore the family, the neighborhood, the community, and the workplace as vital alternatives in our national life to ever-expanding federal power.

The three sections that focused exclusively on the family were:

1. The family is the foundation of our social order. It is the school of democracy. Its daily lessons—cooperation, tolerance, mutual concern, responsibility, industry—are fundamental to the order and progress of our Republic. But the Democrats have shunted the family aside. They have given its power to the bureaucracy, its jurisdiction to the courts, and its resources to government grantors. For the first time in our history, there is real concern that the family may not survive.

   Government may be strong enough to destroy families, but it can never replace them.

   Unlike the Democrats, we do not advocate new federal bureaucracies with ominous power to shape a national family order. Rather, we insist that all domestic policies, from child care and schooling to Social Security and the tax code, must be formulated with the family in mind.

2. It is increasingly common for both husbands and wives to work outside the home. Often, it occurs out of economic necessity, and it creates major difficulties for families with children, especially those of pre-school age. On one hand, they are striving to improve the economic well-being of their family; on the other, they are concerned about the physical and emotional well-being of their children. This dilemma is further aggravated in instances of single parenthood due to death or divorce.

   Recognizing these problems, we pledge to increase the availability of non-institutional child care. We see a special role for local, private organizations in meeting this need.

   We disapprove of the bias in the federal tax system against working spouses, whose combined incomes are taxed at a proportionately higher rate than if they were single. We deplore this ''marriage tax'' and call for equity in the tax treatment of families.

   We applaud our society's increasing awareness of the role of homemakers in the economy, not apart from the work force but as a very special part of it: the part that combines the labor of a full-time job, the skills of a profession, and the commitment of the most dedicated volunteer. Recognizing that homemaking is as important as any other profession, we endorse expanded eligibility for Individual Retirement Accounts for homemakers and will explore other ways to advance their standing and security.

3. In view of the continuing efforts of the present Administration to define and influence the family through such federally funded conferences as the White House Conference on Families, we express our support for legislation protecting and defending the traditional American family against the ongoing erosion of its base in our society.

Many additional sections were family relevant, such as Women's Rights, Abortion, Youth, and the Welfare System. Several sections explicitly included family considerations, such as the following lead paragraph for the section, Handicapped People:

Republicans will seek every effective means to enable families more easily to assist their handicapped members and to provide for their education and special medical and therapeutic needs. In the case of handicapped children particularly, flexibility must be maintained in programs of public assistance so that, whenever possible, these youngsters may remain at home rather than in institutions.

All in all, the Republican platform seemed quite sensitive to the topic of families.

Because of the interest demonstrated in families by President Carter and Vice-President Mondale, one expected to find considerable space devoted to families in the Democratic platform, but that was not the case. Only one section was devoted solely to families and that consisted of the following one-sentence paragraph:

> The Democratic Party supports efforts to make federal programs more sensitive to the needs of the family, in all its diverse forms.

As in the Republican plantform, the Democratic platform contained several sections that were family sensitive; for instance, the following section on long-term care:

> We must develop a new policy on long-term care for our elderly and disabled populations that controls the cost explosion and at the same time provides more humane care. We must establish alternatives to the present provisions for long-term care, including adequate support systems and physical and occupational therapy in the home and the community, to make it unnecessary to institutionalize people who could lead productive lives at home.

Overall, however, the opinion here is that the Democratic attention to families was less explicit and less pervasive than the Republican, which makes detailed comparison somewhat difficult. Clearly the Republicans favored less government and the more traditional family, whereas the Democrats favored federal programs and respect for family pluralism. Both stressed the need to accent home care rather than institutional care. But the unexpected scarcity of detail in the Democratic platform makes further comparisons and contrasts impossible.

Additionally, the family was not a major topic of debate in the Carter/Reagan campaigns. Both candidates took a conservative stance on abortion; Carter advocated passage of the Equal Rights Amendment, whereas Reagan did not. No other family issue received significant attention, except perhaps the all-pervasive issues of inflation and unemployment. Reagan's landslide victory, the passage of control of the Senate to the Republicans, and the defeat at the polls of many liberal Democratic leaders in the House and Senate reflected the general shift of the public to conservative stances such as those that had surfaced during the WHCF process.

The implications of such a wholesale changing of the guard are undoubtedly profound for the immediate future of public family policy, but the precise nature of those implications is not yet clear. Certainly the potential effectiveness of the WHCF is reduced, both because at least two months of its six-month implementation stage will be lost to the transition stage of government transfer of administration and because Republican leadership had been continuously disdainful of the WHCF process, signaling a probable deaf ear to

WHCF recommendations. Similarly the future of the Office for Families, created by President Carter, is understandably uncertain.

Ironically, the WHCF staff seems assured of making its mark. By eliciting such negative responses from many leading Republicans, it helped to sharpen that Party's posture on the topic of family policy. In such alternatives to the WHCF's recommendations as Senator Laxalt's Family Protection Act, it appears likely that short-run public policy will focus sharply on the economic dimension of life in families at and especially above the poverty line, and that the means of such policy will largely be tax breaks and incentives rather than federally sponsored programs. By extension, policy decision-making about programs will probably shift markedly from the federal level to the state level, and attention to the pluralistic nature of American families will probably lessen.

The private sector continued to expand its interest in the family into the fall of 1980. The *Reader's Digest* introduced a new quarterly magazine, *Families;* the Church of Jesus Christ of Latter-Day Saints declared a National Family Week in November. However, the public sector's interest in family policy, although still intense, will remain a matter of conjecture into the near future.

Those who are unfamiliar with the machinations of public policy are disquieted by the on-again, off-again nature of policy initiatives, the painfully slow progress, the inefficiencies, the continuous clash of rival ideologies, and discontinuities occasioned by changes in administration. However, such is our political and administrative system, and expectations beyond its capabilities yield only frustration. The system is not capable of perfection and many have concluded it is not capable of efficiency. Yet the cumulative impact on families of its actions and inactions is so profound as to make paramount any and all efforts to help the policy system realize its maximum potential for rationality and effectiveness.

Chapter 6

Scientific and Professional Modeling

All those who contribute to the policy development and implementation process bring with them basic orientations to the world that allow them to define some things as problems and other things as solutions. Much of this orientation is unconscious, arising from innumerable exposures to the culture surrounding them, and much of it is idiosyncratic, resulting from deeply personal, highly meaningful experiences. But much of it, especially among professionals, is brought explicitly from modes of conceptualization developed in various professional and scientific communities. These are structured ways of looking at the world that simplify complex reality along carefully selected dimensions and that help policy analysis to be explicit, rational, and communicable.

Unfortunately, studying how people conceptualize reality in structured ways has not been a popular academic activity. Most professions are quite parochial about their modes of conceptualization, so that there is no study across disciplines that attempts to lay out the set of explicit models that can be brought to bear on family policy analysis. Yet, the effort is quite important if policy analysis is to become more visibly systematic, more objectively assessed, and more measurably productive.

The pages that follow are an attempt to lay out some of the existing conceptual models that have been or could be used in family policy analysis. The models to be discussed are far from a complete set and are only intended to demonstrate the variety of conceptual models that one might find in use at any given time. The models inherent in the earlier discussion of professional and scientific knowledge of the family have not been reiterated here. These models focus principally on ways of understanding the family and its problems, and on ways of treating troubled families. The available literature is encyclopedic in size; its omission here in no way reflects a low opinion of it, but rather a need to be brief and to avoid being redundant.

The models are randomly ordered below, followed by an integrative discussion and summary.

A SIMPLE DICHOTOMY MODEL

Robert Leik and Reuben Hill (1979) offer the simplest and clearest twofold classification of policy options by distinguishing between problems internal to the family and problems external to it.

> A quest for optimal policy can be aided by a few simple distinctions. First, one must decide whether the policy is focused on conditions *affecting* families or conditions *of* families. The former has to do with such factors as national or local level of unemployment. The latter refers to individual family factors such as financial adequacy, mutual emotional supportiveness, or ability to care for and nurture children. The distinction, then, is between an external (conditions affecting) versus internal (conditions of) locus of the problems addressed by the policy.

The value of this distinction is that it goes one step beyond the necessary first step of understanding problems *of* families; until that is accomplished, it is impossible to distinguish between problems arising within the family and problems resulting from external pressures on it, or some combination.

Professions that treat families with problems do well at understanding problems *of* families irrespective of their origins. Such professions, when they advocate policy changes, frequently press for larger treatment systems to do a better job for all in need. Such professions, however, may underestimate the larger societal forces that contribute to the formation of treatable family problems and, consequently, frequently do not advocate policy changes that focus on those external forces.

On the other hand, those who specialize in broad social conditions too frequently omit family impact from their considerations. As Leik and Hill put it:

> Major conditions affecting families tend to be large scale and best handled at national or possibly state or regional levels of government. The level of unemployment and the extent of the economic squeeze due to inflation or the interest rate on mortgages are obvious examples of conditions which local communities can affect very little but which the federal government can and does affect continuously. It is not often asked how policies in these areas will impinge on the nation's families, yet those efforts can be far more drastic than, for instance, the effects of a new dam on some local environment. There is, in fact, considerable interest at the state and national levels in family impact analysis for a potential use as a guide to making family policy.

Obviously policy analysts must have the breadth of vision to encompass the full scope of family problems, their origins, and their consequences. Otherwise some options for fruitful planning may be missed. Also—and this is an opinion not shared by all—policy analysts should be multidisciplinary in their orientation, because no one science is completely adequate for an understanding of the many dimensions of family problems and the various forms of governmental responses to them. Therefore, policy analysis is probably the most intellectually demanding career available to professionals today.

THE PUBLIC HEALTH AND GOAL ATTAINMENT MODELS

The field of public health was one of the first to develop a classification scheme for all of its activities, proposing several decades ago the fourfold classification of promotion, prevention, treatment, and rehabilitation.

Promotion stands alone as being oriented to advancing health rather than responding to illness. Diet control and exercise are two "promotion" activities intended to advance health.

Prevention is intended to reduce the extent of pathology in a population, focusing on the etiology or causes of disease more than on the disease itself. Two subclassifications further define preventive activities. The first divides them by purpose: 1) there are those activities that remove causative factors from the environment, such as purifying the air or enforcing food processing regulations to keep disease-causing organisms from getting into the food in the first place; 2) there are those activities that reduce the likelihood that potentially disease- or injury-producing factors will exact their full toll, such as requiring workers to wear protective gear when handling dangerous chemicals or educating the public about the dangers of warming their cars with the garage door shut; and 3) there are those activities that interrupt a disease process early enough to keep it from reaching its full destructive potential, such as treating hypertension before it leads to cardiac arrest or surgically removing a small tumor before it grows and spreads throughout the body. The second subclassification scheme focuses on the interactions among man, his environment, and (in the case of disease more so than injury) pathological organisms; there are 1) those activities that focus on protecting man, such as immunizing him against polio, 2) those activities that purify man's environment, such as removing the type of mosquito that carries malarial sporozoan parasites, and 3) those activities that keep pathological agents from entering man's environment or spreading in it, such as the isolation of persons with infectious diseases.

Treatment is the best known health activity, since virtually every profession and every service system traces its origins to the need to respond therapeutically to various diseases or problems and because virtually everyone has had the experience of being treated for something.

Rehabilitation occurs after treatment or concurrently with it. It is an attempt to restore, to the degree possible, functional capacities that were lost as a result of disease or injury. These activities range from providing prostheses to retraining persons for new jobs within their remaining capacities.

The set of promotion/prevention/treatment/rehabilitation (PPTR) activities includes all possible public health activities and, by clustering them in four large sets, provides a bird's-eye view of an otherwise overwhelmingly complex network of thousands of specific health activities. The popularity of this public health model has waned in recent years because of the proliferation of competing models of narrower scope that generally have the advantage of being more useful for specific tasks and the disadvantage of providing less of a comprehensive overview.

A more recent model, the goal attainment model, is not only compatible with the PPTR model but enriches it by being comprehensive along a different dimension. This model, described by Deniston, Rosenstock, and Gettings (1968), maintains that any human endeavor must be understood in terms of resources, activities, and goals. The *activities* are, like the verb in a sentence, the action taken or the work done; the PPTR model specifies activities, not goals or resources. The *resources,* like the subject in a sentence, describe who did the work and also include money, equipment, and time used to perform the activities. The *goals,* like the object in a sentence, describe the impact of the activities—the desired effect of the activities.

Combining the goal attainment model with the PPTR model creates a powerful tool for policy planning and analysis. Policy is first and foremost concerned with goals—the identification of how one wants things to be as contrasted with how they are. And since PPTR is an exhaustive list of general activities, one may reason from it to an exhaustive list of general goals. The goal of promotion activities is a high level of health, a full capacity for robust living. The goals of prevention are eliminating or reducing disease-causing forces and nipping pathological processes in the bud. The goals of treatment are the cure or stabilization of disease and the alleviation of suffering. The goal of rehabilitation is the restoration of functioning. All other goals are refinements or more specific applications of these four:

Production and maintenance of high level of health
Elimination or reduction of disease-causing forces and early intervention in
    pathological processes
Cure or stabilization of disease and alleviation of suffering
Restoration of functioning

Given goals, the planning and evaluation of activities may become more explicitly rational. Two or more different activities may be capable of attaining the same goal. Given the goal of reducing the number of fatal auto accidents in a county—a specific prevention goal—one may identify the potentially preventive activities of putting more patrol cars on the most dangerous roads, requiring more frequent auto inspections, increasing the penalties for convicted violators, or increasing the drinking age, to name a few. The criteria used for selecting one or more activities for implementation will include at least effectiveness (will it work?) and appropriateness (can government do that?).

Given selected activities, the planning and evaluation of resources becomes more explicitly rational. Two or more resources may be appropriate for a given activity. To attain the goal of a successful convalescence at home following major surgery, the selected activities of controlling the diet carefully and maintaining an exercise schedule might be performed by the trained patient or by a home health aide or by a visiting nurse from the health department, or by some combination of resources. The criteria used to select the resource may be efficiency (which costs less?) and consumer preference (what do the patient and his family want?).

It should be evident that these three simple concepts—resources, activities, and goals—can be extended into a rather complex and detailed examination of human endeavor.

Plotting the two models against each other yields some interesting new information, especially for the combinations of resources and PPTR activities. "Promotion" is principally within the control of the individual person and the individual family. How they eat and recreate and relate to each other are principal determinants of how physically and emotionally robust they are. Health education may make them more efficient and effective at it, but the ultimate choice is the individual's. "Prevention" is partly within the control of the individual and the family. Whether they smoke or drink or abuse drugs determines their health risks, as may their driving habits, their sexual practices, and their safety consciousness; individuals and families are in a commanding position to prevent or cause health problems. However, they are also dependent upon the preventive activities of professionals in and out of government—the sanitary engineers who keep the water clean, the doctors and nurses who immunize children, the occupational safety experts. Prevention is a shared responsibility between the individual and organized society. "Treatment," of course, is principally dependent upon the medical professions, and the individual and her family are, or should be, active collaborators. "Rehabilitation," similarly, draws on the skills of physicians, vocational rehabilitation counselors, social workers, and physical therapists, to name a few, with the patient and his family active collaborators.

Forcing oneself to use models such as these reduces the likelihood of errors of omission. For instance, the most persistent pressure for changes in public policy comes from the "service system," wherein professionals are so aware of needed changes that they often tend to limit their advocacy to self-serving ends. This may result in too little attention to consumer needs for self-initiatives and self-help, especially in the area of promotion, an understandable but regrettable phenomenon. Somewhat similarly, the service systems tend to be organized around treatment activities, and it is not unusual for disease-causing forces to be out of their control, which makes prevention difficult. Those treating emotionally disturbed children, for instance, do not control the educational system, which may have practices that are emotionally injurious to large numbers of children, but that are helpful with regard to various other educational goals. It is all too easy to confine one's attention to the pressing treatment responsibilities at hand because they are indeed pressing and because collaborative relationships with one's peers in another system for preventive purposes are frequently ineffective or unrewarded by the upper echelons of the employing system. Forcing the model onto the system forces inattention to prevention to the conscious fore.

All of this tends to become quite complex when one gets down to specifics, which is another plus for using models. They simplify the complex to the most important dimensions and, if everyone learns the same models, communication among people and collaborative planning become more feasible. Elaborate, technical refinements are available for detailed work, especially of a research nature, but the basic concepts and vocabulary are easily mastered.

Individually and together, the PPTR and goal attainment models seem as applicable to "the family" as to "public health" insofar as conceptualization goes. They force one to think of the full range of promotion/prevention/treatment/rehabilitation activities as policy options and they force one to set goals and rationally select activities and resources. Using them to analyze existing programs helps to quickly spot overloading in one area of PPTR and deficiencies in another, and it helps to detect malnourished elements in the goal/activity/resource selection process.

Yet the fit is not perfect. In health, mortality and all forms of disease and injury are defined as problems by consumer and provider, public and private sector. Ill health is *bad*. That is a value judgment shared by all and it makes goal-setting rather simple. There is no such consensus on all aspects of family life in terms of what is considered good and bad. Living together without benefit of ceremony is deemed good by some and bad by others. A divorce may be deemed necessary and constructive by one person and unnecessary and destructive by another. There is no consensus about whether abortion is good or bad either in all cases or in specific ones. And on and on. There are many legal types of families, and people, for the most part, are legally entitled to define things as problems or not. And government is required to respect those legal rights.

All of this makes goal setting for family policy rather difficult as compared to that for health. The models are still useful for general conceptualization for the reasons stated above, but the goal-setting component requires much more individualization.

LEVEL OF INTERVENTION STRATEGY

All intervention strategies are, or certainly should be, predicated on a clear statement of the problem. The strength of the preceding models lies in their comprehensiveness and in the cardinal prerequisite to comprehensiveness, simplicity; the basic concepts are few and mirror natural human mental sets. However, their weakness is that they do not provide a structure for defining the problem so that goals may be set and interventions planned. Although such models are legion, there is still ample room at present for innovation, and one such effort is offered here that seems consistent with the general tone of contemporary scientific literature and many types of existing models, especially systems models.

In both professional circles and public opinion there seems to be a growing awareness of forces surrounding the family that affect its well-being, in contrast to healthy and pathological processes within the family. Such models structure their understanding of the family in such a way as to classify these forces and, by so doing, the alternative intervention strategies that policymakers must address. Such a structure is arbitrarily offered in pyramidal fashion in Figure 1.

Some of the forces in Figure 1 are destructive and originate from levels above and below the family. Some of these are brought to the family from its immediate members: the husband who becomes psychotic, the wife who develops cancer, the adolescent who becomes pregnant, the third grader who fails, the grandparent who is physically assaulted on the street—all of these individual problems impact on other members of the immediate family and on the functioning of the family as a whole. Some pressures are brought to the family from its extended kinship system—meddlesome uncle, the alcoholic aunt, the scandalous cousin. Not even families of presidents are immune from these problems.

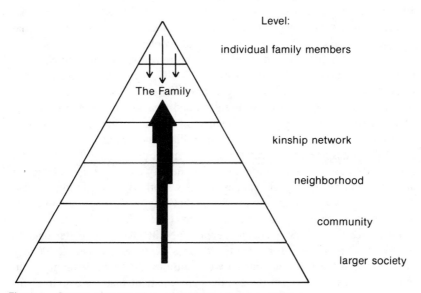

Figure 1.   Sources of constructive and destructive forces on families.

Some pressures originate in the immediate neighborhood—the noisy tenant in the apartment overhead, the neighbor who feeds poisoned meat to your dog, the vandalous youths, the rumbling trucks, the drug pusher. Some pressures originate in the surrounding community—joblessness, urban decay, violence, air pollution, inadequate police protection, poor public transportation—and some pressures originate in the broader society—inflation, inadequate federal and state policies, changing values that conflict with family values, rising home mortgage rates, war.

The other side of the coin, of course, is that many of these forces support the family. Individuals in the immediate family bring extraordinary strength and good will to each other. There is the reassuring feeling from knowing that you can always get a helping hand from Aunt Lucy. There is the helpful, cooperative neighbor in the quiet, safe neighborhood. Fortunate are those who live in communities with adequate recreational facilities, a competent support service system, active civic and social and religious groups, and full employment. In the larger society are inputs of hordes of people and organizations who work on a sound economy, responsive government, healthy entertainment, high quality education, justice, and reasonably priced agricultural products.

How all of the constructive and destructive forces cumulatively impact on any given family is difficult to determine except in extreme cases, yet they self-evidently do impact on all families daily.

This model, expectedly, has its limitations. By focusing on the forces that impact on the family, it ignores the forces internal to the family that result from the interactions of its members, even though these forces are nearly always exacerbated or neutralized by external forces. Therefore it omits most of the variables of concern to treatment professions that specialize in the identification and resolution of conflicts and problems within the family. By extension, it amplifies only that half of the aforementioned simple dichotomy model that deals with the environment. Finally, since the model assumes meaning only in the context of influencing family strengths and weaknesses, it begs the question of what those strengths and weaknesses are and how they are affected by external forces; refinement of the model, therefore, is dependent upon the quality of modeling intrafamilial functioning.

Yet it does seem to be compatible with most parts of the PPTR model, particularly prevention and promotion. By identifying forces that strengthen and support the family, it suggests policy options that reinforce those forces—*promotion.* By identifying forces that may weaken some families, it suggests policy options that remove or temper those forces—*prevention.* In terms of *treatment,* although the model provides little help with understanding the nature of problems *in* the family, it forces treatment planners to identify environmental pressures that intensify or neutralize the treatable family problem as well as elements in the family's environment that are resources for developing and implementing a treatment plan. The same holds true for *rehabilitation.*

Clearly the model is more useful for conceptualization than for quantitative analysis, since measuring the impact of environmental variables becomes more difficult as one moves from the immediate environment of the family. For instance, the work of Brenner (1976) shows a general statistical association between the state of the economy and various social problems, such as the rate of mental institutionalization. Important as such data are for general policy considerations, they provide little insight into the dynamics of the relationship of broad social forces and family problems, and no insight at all into the origin of a specific family's problem.

The model clearly differentiates between individual and family strengths and weaknesses, which goes beyond much contemporary thinking, especially with regard to treatment. The model clearly isolates problems individuals have as individual problems, and they unquestionably should be understood as such; yet the model features those problems of individuals as stressors on the larger family and that added dimension is equally important.

The model is quite compatible with the notion of control. The family is clearly capable of establishing controls over its immediate environment. It can, in many instances, modify the emerging deviant behavior of an adolescent member or take cousin Shirley's handicapped child for a week so she and her husband can get away for a rest. To a lesser degree they can improve the quality of the neighborhood and draw on it for help, but the degree of control is less. In the community and larger society, controls are even less total and are exercised in forms such as voting, participating in civic associations, and boycotting certain goods and establishments. Consequently, whereas families can and do establish controls over their immediate environs, they are much more dependent on other forces, such as sound public policy, for influencing the larger environment in such matters as inflation control, drug flow control, and discriminatory employment control.

Finally, the model is humbling for the self-aggrandizing policy analyst because it puts implemented policy in the context of being just one more force in the family's environment rather than casting the policy analyst as the godlike overseer of the big picture, tinkering here and there to effect desirable changes. Also, as suggested above, it makes the policy analyst consider high priority for general environmental changes, such as legislating against discrimination, because these are not within the control of the family and, therefore, if policymakers fail, few other societal forces exist to come to the rescue.

SYSTEMS ANALYSIS

On his way to the nose capsule for the first moonshot, one of the astronauts got the chills when he realized that the whole space ship had been assembled from the work of low bidders. That the mission was successful is proof that an enormously complex endeavor can succeed by first being broken down into smaller, simpler, more manageable parts and then being reassembled into a functional whole. The management term for this process is systems analysis.

The federal bureaucracy in many ways resembles the first step in the process, breaking the complex whole into smaller parts. The total federal effort is broken down administratively into the broad areas of health, education, welfare, labor, housing, and so on. Each of these, in turn, is broken down into smaller and smaller units to the level of specific management responsibilities. Although there are ample grounds for quarreling with the *way* government has done this, one must admit that it has, in fact, broken a terribly complex total effort down into parts of manageable size.

The principal deficiency of government has been in the second half of the process—assembling the manageable parts into a functional whole. Smooth working agreements among administratively distant parts are few, generally short-lived, and frequently accidental. The importance of the integrative function in systems analysis is so great that many federal analysts prefer to delegate it to the states; the usual procedure is to require state agencies who receive federal funds to submit a state plan showing how the activities resulting from those funds will be integrated with the activities resulting from other federal funds in related areas.

This whole topic has an interesting twist when it comes to family policy. Nearly all the thinking about family policy has been limited to the parts, with relatively little attention to the whole except for the gut feeling that surely there should be a total family policy rather than random, uncoordinated efforts here and there. However, most of the detailed work on the family has focused on various dimensions of the family, especially family problems—marital discord, abuse, financial dependency, abortion, disability, and a host of others. Yet little work has been done on aggregating these dimensions into larger and more comprehensive conceptualizations of the family to which an overall family policy can be fit. Indeed, there are those who hold that such an overall family policy is not possible, so that we will have to content ourselves with a set of policies for the parts without an overall guiding philosophy.

Additionally, even an overall family policy is no more than part of the total federal system and should be compatible with other parts of that system insofar as that is possible. Many of the parts of the current system reflect a deliberate or unconscious preoccupation with the well-being of individuals that may result in conflicts with the well-being of the family, and vice versa. The family that attempts to restrain an adolescent member from having an abortion may find itself in conflict with members of the judicial and medical systems who are committed to protecting the adolescent's rights and may not be sensitive to the needs and desires of the rest of the family. Or, families who are quite happy with their homes and neighborhoods may be displaced by urban renewal or road construction, which are serving the "common good."

In short, systems analysis models require a logical balance between the whole and the parts, but family policy in the short run will likely be preoccupied with the parts. Earlier models can help to identify which parts (options) are attended to and which are unattended.

The language of systems analysis corresponds very closely to the concepts and language of the goal attainment model described above. *Input* is a systems term that corresponds to the concept of *resources* in the goal attainment (GA) model. Two systems terms correspond to the concept of *activity* in the GA model; *throughput* refers to the entire process of completing an activity and *output* refers to the completed work. It becomes necessary to distinguish between output and desired *outcome* (*goal,* in the GA model) when there is less than complete certainty that the output will attain the desired outcome. For instance, the output from a physician's "system" for a patient with an infection may be a patient with a prescription for antibiotics. However, whether the patient has the prescription filled and whether the antibiotics truly "work" are not within the physician's control; therefore the outcome (cured infection) may not be realized from the output (a correctly diagnosed patient with a prescription for the appropriate medicine).

The author has done considerable work cross-referencing the concepts in various management and evaluation models, and has found them to be extraordinarily compatible. The sheer number of terms, however, does tend to become burdensome, and further cross-referencing is not attempted here.

PRIORITIZATION

Prioritization, in some respects, is the antithesis of systems analysis because it reflects the judgment that we can't do it all, so we'll accent some of the parts—the most important ones. It reflects limited resources or other constraints, and therefore is primarily economic in its thinking.

Prioritization proceeds in two stages. First, all of one's options for attaining a policy goal are listed and, second, one applies evaluative criteria to the options in order to rank them according to desirability. Listing the options usually depends on some other model such as the PPTR or Level of Intervention models. For instance, one may have authority to plan policy for a full range of promotion/prevention/treatment/rehabilitation activities, but have only half the funds to do it all. So prioritization among these four alternatives may be deemed necessary.

Given the options or alternatives, evaluative criteria are applied. Some of these are explicit. *Appropriateness for government* is one criterion; it might seem that the well-being of families would be promoted if more people went to church regularly, yet it is not appropriate for government to attempt to influence church-going behavior. It is customary to rank options by *expected effectiveness*—which options are most likely to have the desired effects and which are not so likely? Options are also ranked by *cost*—with equal expected effectiveness among options, which are least costly? *Number of people affected* is another criterion. *Mandates* must be considered—Congress or the courts may require some options to be included among the final selections by policy analysts in the executive branch.

Finally, there is the criterion of *principles*. Some principles are rather simple: when faced with a choice between prevention and treatment, always choose prevention first if its expected effectiveness is high. Some of the principles are more complex, such as the minimax principle (Reinke, 1972). This principle assumes that every activity will have both positive and negative effects; expanding infant day care programs in a community will allow more women to work who really need to for the economic well-being of the family (positive effect), but it also increases the risk of periodic outbreaks of communicable diseases, such as infectious hepatitis (negative effect). One then selects the option or options that give the best combination of positive and negative effects. (Like many of the models above, there are several techniques to make the minimax principle a quantitative procedure, but even then the procedure is still controlled by the subjective estimates of the decision maker, since hard data are rarely available for all parts of the formula.)

Even under the best of circumstances, there are always implicit criteria in the prioritization process that are unconscious or are not entirely virtuous. There is the squeaky wheel criterion; it is difficult to ignore the demands of the loudest, and some wizened bureaucrats candidly credit their survival to applying this criterion freely to their options. There is the criterion of personal preference; many people get into the "system" because of an intense commitment to a given policy option and press for it even though the needs of the system would be better served by other options. There is the line-of-least-resistance criterion; no one individual makes policy without the laying on of hands all along the bureaucratic process, so that some select the option they think has the best chance of making it—it's only human to want to have something to show for one's labor. And there are all the other less virtuous criteria—personal gain, returning favors, and so on—that are publicized enough that they need no amplification here.

Since government never has enough money to do it all, prioritization is virtually a continuous activity in every branch of government and at all levels. Too infrequently does it take place explicitly and openly so that all may observe it, yet rationalizing the process is essential to sound policy development. It seems impossible to underestimate the importance of this process.

NARROW, SPECIFIC MODELS

Many models are narrow in contrast to the global models above, and some are only tangentially related to the family. Yet, they are important because they are the conceptual orientations many professionals bring with them to family policy analysis. Four are discussed briefly here from the fields/professions of child welfare, education, disability, and sociology because they have enjoyed more than a little popularity, because they are quite compatible with each other, and because they illustrate the degree to which existing models are or are not compatible with family policy analysis.

Child Welfare Model

Kadushin (1974) has long been the proponent of a service model for the child welfare field that uniquely conceptualizes the welfare of children in the context of their families. He maintains that there are three principal role relationships in the family (husband-wife, parent-child, and sibling) and problems in any one of these may adversely affect the children. Consequently he poses seven major problems of role functioning in the parent-child relationship, each of which has several manifestations:

1. Parental role unoccupied because of death of parent, hospitalization, or imprisonment.
2. Parental incapacity as a result of illness, physical handicap, ignorance, or emotional immaturity.
3. Parental role rejection through neglect, abandonment, or desertion.
4. Role conflict between parents with regard to definition of role or definition of role behavior.
5. Conflict between parental and other roles.
6. Child incapacity and/or handicap, resulting in excessive demand.
7. Deficiency of community resources.

(This list is a simplification and modification of Kadushin's list in the interest of brevity.)

Having classified the major types of role performance problems in the family, Kadushin proceeds to classify services in a priority trilogy. First priority (referred to as the first line of defense) is accorded to those services that are intended to strengthen the role relationships in the family that are under strain. For the most part this consists of counseling/psychiatric/ casework services. The second priority, given the failure of the first line of defense, is accorded to services that participate in or assume some family roles. Income maintenance, homemaker services, and day care programs are examples of this second line of defense. Given the failure of even these services, the third line of defense may be the total assumption of family roles relative to the child in such forms as foster care, institutional care, or adoption. The terms for these three gradations of interventions are *supportive, supplementary,* and *substitute* services. These three gradations are not necessarily on a scale of severity of role impairment, but are three points on a scale of degree of assumption of family roles. The selection of a service from alternatives follows the principle that one should intervene as little as possible, but as much as is necessary; that is, support services—if possible—should be given priority over supplementary services, and supplementary services—if possible—should be given priority over substitute services. A second principle is that services over time should move toward supportive services and finally, if possible, to withdrawal of service.

Plotting the role functioning problems against the prioritized trilogy of supportive/supplementary/substitute services yields an interesting matrix (see Table 5). All child welfare services should fit in one of the cells of the matrix, which makes the model elegant (simple and comprehensive) and useful. For instance, if one examines a child welfare budget and finds a heavy investment in substitute services of various types, the model forces one to ask whether this reflects need or whether it may reflect too little attention to supportive and supplementary services that would reduce the need for substitute services. (Only a few sample services have been included in the cells of Table 5; filling in the remaining cells is recommended to test the model's elegance and to gain familiarity with it.)

The Normalization Principle

The normalization principle originated in Scandinavia as a guiding force for providing service to the mentally retarded, and has been defined as "... making available to the mentally retarded patterns and conditions of everyday life

Table 5. Matrix of child welfare services; role functioning problems by service type

Role functioning problems	Service types: priority		
	Supportive	Supplementary	Substitute
1. Parental role unoccupied			
2. Parental incapacity		homemaker service	
3. Parental role rejection			adoption
4. Role conflict between parents	counseling		
5. Conflict between parental and other roles			
6. Child incapacity and/or handicap			
7. Deficiency of community resources			

which are as close as possible to the norms and patterns of the mainstream of society'' (Nirje, 1969). The principle is seen as applicable to all gradations of severity of retardation, to all ages, and to those living at home or in institutions.

The normalization principle was introduced to the United States in the late 1960s with Wolf Wolfensberger as its chief proponent. Interestingly, he states (1970) that his first reaction to the principle was one of disinterest, since it tends to state the obvious—a reaction shared by many. It begins to take on meaning when it is contrasted with life in low-quality service systems, especially in the worst institutions for which, when one thinks about it, the criterion of ''badness'' is denormalization. For many persons it appears that the principle of normalization is acceptable because its opposite is intolerable.

Court-ordered treatment in the least restrictive setting and the entire deinstitutionalization movement are justified by the principle of normalization. An impairment or disability is just one dimension of a human being, so that treatment that disturbs all respects of living ''denormalizes'' the person. The principle seems quite applicable to families. Most people live in families and those who plan services should consider keeping the person with a problem in his normal family setting and allowing family members to participate in the care spontaneously. Too much institutional care, especially in nursing homes, is for the convenience of the provider and neglects the preferences of the patient as well as the strengths and willingness of the family members.

The principle of normalization is quite compatible with the child welfare principle of according priority to supporting ''normal'' family roles over supplementing them or substituting for them altogether.

Special Education and the Mainstreaming Principle

Reynolds (1962) wrote a special education article several years ago that is still extensively quoted, in which he develops a simple, graphic model of service for children with educational problems (see Figure 2). The bottom row of this figure contains the multitude of problems of low severity that are handled routinely in the regular classroom. The ascending rows form an ordinal scale of educational services and placements that are increasingly distant from the regular classroom. The principle governing the selection of service placement is that any given child should be removed from the regular classroom only as far as is necessary and should be returned as soon as possible. If this principle is truly practiced, the frequency distribution of children in placements should resemble a triangle, with the fewest number of cases in the setting most distant from the regular classroom.

In recent years the term ''mainstreaming'' has been applied to this concept of service. Unfortunately, it has been misinterpreted by many, and the Council for Exceptional Children has found it necessary to publish the following explanatory definition (''What is 'Mainstreaming'?'', 1975):

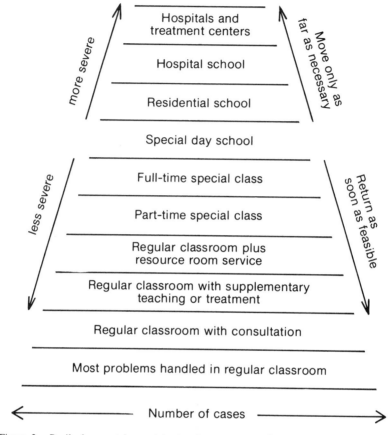

Figure 2. Pupil placement in special education programs. (Reprinted by permission from: Reynolds, M. C. A framework for considering some issues in special education. *Exceptional Children 28*, 376–380, 1962. Copyright 1962 by The Council for Exceptional Children.)

The term "mainstreaming" has been used frequently and in different ways during the last few years. Along with its varied meanings has come confusion regarding what the word really means. While there may not be a definition that is universally agreed on, there are some basic themes that can be looked to for an understanding of the intent of mainstreaming.

Mainstreaming is:

—providing the most appropriate education for each child in the least restrictive setting.

—looking at the educational needs of children instead of clinical or diagnostic labels such as mentally handicapped, learning disabled, physically handicapped, hearing impaired or gifted.

—looking for and creating alternatives that will help general educators serve children with learning or adjustment problems in the regular setting. Some approaches being used to achieve this are consulting teachers, methods and materials specialists, itinerant teachers and resource room teachers.

—uniting the skills of general education and special education so that all children may have equal educational opportunity.

Mainstreaming is not:

—wholesale return of all exceptional children in special classes to regular classes.

—permitting children with special needs to remain in regular classrooms without the support services that they need.

—ignoring the need of some children for a more specialized program that can be provided in the general education program.

—less costly than serving children in special self-contained classrooms.

Although mainstreaming has not yet been completely accepted among educators, it permeates Public Law 94-142 (Education for All Handicapped Children Act, November, 1975) and has been cautiously endorsed by the National Education Association's representative assembly.

The mainstreaming principle is in complete harmony with the normalization principle since it features keeping students with problems as close as possible to their "normal" educational setting. However, it is not a family model, reflecting instead in-house educational decisions. It becomes a family model only when parents are included in the planning process.

It is also compatible with the child welfare model, which facilitates collaboration between systems. A child with several problems may simultaneously come to the attention of the educational system and the child welfare system. With one system attempting to maintain him in his normal family setting and the other attempting to maintain him in the mainstream of normal education, the common philosophical orientation in the two systems may facilitate intersystem collaboration between professionals who otherwise are strangers to each other.

Sociology and Disability

In the "Disability" section in Chapter 3, sociologists were shown to view disability as a role performance failure in the context of the performance expectations of the disabled person's environment. Haber and Smith (1971) have expanded that viewpoint to a conceptual model of the steps society goes through to legitimize the role performance deficiency and to "manage" it.

The initial premise is that service agencies have the power and ability to confer or deny legitimacy to behavior. Therefore, three initial stages are identified in the process of legitimizing incapacity:

1. Recognition of a change in behavior as a role-relevant failure of performance.
2. Attribution of responsibility for incapacity to a condition or impairment beyond the control of the individual.

3. Legitimation of the performance failure by an appropriate agency of social control . . . (by) separating the compliant disabled from the willful deviant.

After the legitimation of performance failure, the service system has a logically finite number of ways of intervening to manage the effects of incapacity, according to Haber and Smith:

1. removing or adjusting the impairment, to permit a return to conventional expectations;
2. adjusting the (person), through the addition of new or improved capacities;
3. adjusting the situation, through changes in the role requirements or the environment to fit existing capacities; or
4. providing alternative systems for obtaining need satisfactions, such as income replacement or institutional care.

The entire process of legitimation and role maintenance is seen as the normalization of incapacity, and therefore it is completely compatible with the concept of normalization as stated above. The model is focused on individuals rather than families, but it is not incompatible with a family orientation, especially when the role performance deficiency affects the family.

Discussion

Three of the four narrow models above focus entirely on disability and the fourth (child welfare) encompasses it. Although some focus on the family and some do not, and although they are adapted to different fields of service (e.g., education and child welfare), they are all essentially compatible. Because of this, people with different backgrounds are able to work together on policy analysis without necessarily being fully conversant with each other's modes of conceptualizations and vocabularies.

Additionally, for a given policy "problem" there may be no one conceptualization model that "fits" perfectly. For such a problem the skilled policy analyst must amalgamate whatever set of narrow models is needed to approach the problem systematically. Sometimes a single person can accomplish this; other times, a team of specialists is required. The degree of compatibility of available models determines part of the potential for such analysis, as does the integration skill of the individual analyst or team of specialists.

UTOPIAN MODELS

In his award-winning book, *The New Utopians,* Boguslaw (1965) described four approaches to system design; although he does not address government-supported systems, his comments are relevant to them. Usually a system employs more than one approach, but Boguslaw discusses them separately.

The first is the *formalist* approach, which employs models. This approach requires a relatively uncomplicated situation in which the manager has control over the essential ingredients in the system and in which unanticipated complications are unlikely. Maintaining adequate supplies in a hospital with a computer-assisted inventory model would be one example. Building a house is another. Still another would be to operate a graduate training program in family policy. Formal goal setting is possible and necessary in this approach. The goal attainment model is an example of this approach.

The second type of system design is the *heuristic* approach, which uses principles to guide action. This is a particularly useful approach in unstable, changing situations in which the attainability of goals varies continuously and in which the system design does not have control over all the forces of change. Many of the models above use the heuristic approach—for example, the normalization principle and the minimax principle.

The *operating unit* approach employs neither models nor principles. "It begins with people or machines carefully selected . . . to possess certain performance characteristics. The system or organization or utopia that ultimately unfolds will incorporate solutions that these units provide." In other words, if you parachuted a physician and a nurse into some undeveloped country and simply told them to do something, it is more likely that they would start a medical clinic than a hobby shop, since that is what they have been "programmed" to do. Performance is predictable.

Finally, the *ad hoc* approach does not use models or principles or operating units. It starts with the here and now of an existing system and modifies it to bring it closer to standard. Some people refer to this as the incremental approach to system design, and it is used to some degree in all on-going systems.

"On-going federal programs constantly effect *incremental changes* to enhance the likelihood of attaining *goals,* the nature of the change sometimes being suggested by *principles* which are *predictably* interpreted by programmed policy analysts." From this one sentence it is evident that elements of the four approaches are to be found in virtually all on-going federal programs. Recognizing that helps one to understand what approaches *are* and *are not* consciously operating in a system, thereby helping to make the process more rational.

DISCUSSION AND SUMMARY

Few policymakers and policy analysts are trained for their work. Few have ever taken a course on public policy or read a book on the subject, although attorneys do tend to receive the most relevant education insofar as all public policy must have a legislative base. Lobbyists and advocates tend to grow into their roles, and policy analysts are generally hired because of technical or substantive expertise of use to the policy process. Without a common professional culture about public policy to link them together, it becomes essential to understand the orientations policy actors bring with them so that we may understand the policymaking process that does in fact exist.

All of the models described above come from the scientific or professional community, which is only one input to the policymaking process. Yet, next to nothing is known about how these collective conceptual orientations are brought to bear on policy issues. Consequently the scientific contribution to policymaking and analysis is largely what Boguslaw (1965) called the operating unit approach to system design—the spontaneous outpouring of the conceptual orientations of policy actors, the spontaneous outpouring of what the actors have been programmed to contribute. Whether this approach to designing a "policy system" is the best type of design has not yet even been raised as an issue.

Some of the models described in this or previous chapters help to "define the problem" for policymakers; they aid the understanding of families, the understanding of family problems and the sources of those problems, and the estimation of what might be done appropriately, effectively, and efficiently. Some of the models help to understand government—the interrelatedness of the several branches and levels. Some of the models help the understanding of what systems (governmental and other) are and how they operate and how they may be managed. Many of the models offer principles that provide general guidelines for action. Some of the models help to clarify what one's policy options are; these are especially helpful for understanding what you are doing and what you are *not* doing, thereby reducing the likelihood of accidental errors of omission. Some of the models are more useful for policy planning; some, for policy implementation; some, for policy evaluation. Some of the models are already focused on the family and others must be adapted to it.

The models described here and in earlier sections are a small sampler of all the models policy actors are in fact using today. It is an obscurely understood process that needs to become more explicit if it is to be systematically improved. Only one thing is certain. An era of family policy development has begun. The direction it takes will in large measure result from whatever scientific and conceptual orientations key actors bring to the task. The needs of society will be best served if the underlying modes of conceptualization are explicit and highly visible.

A substantial segment of society reacts negatively to "modeling"—just another unproductive, egg-head pastime. The opinion here, however, is that few other activities have more utilitarian value than understanding how humans in this society think about the family and government's responsibilities for it. Improvements in the quality of the policy formation/implementation process will likely start here.

Chapter 7

Summary, Discussion, and Prognostications

SUMMARY

The American family has changed so dramatically over the centuries that there is little similarity between colonial and contemporary families in size, composition, longevity, scope of function, division of labor among members, and homogeneity of life-styles. Equally dramatic has been the transition of government from the dominance of townships to the sprawling federal bureaucracy. And equally dramatic has been the increasingly intimate impact of the federal government on the daily family experience in terms of payroll deductions, cost of food, emission controls on cars, income transfer payments (Social Security, AFDC), regulated services (day care, hospitals), road conditions, laws governing individual behavior (abortions), drug traffic control, inflation rates, the cost of higher education, warnings on packs of cigarettes, minimum wages, draft registration, and so on.

In spite of this intimate association between government activity and the family experience, explicit consideration of the situation has occurred only within the past three decades, mainly because European pioneering efforts jarred us into a sense of oversight. Early interest was limited to the professional/scientific community, wherein members had long had a clinical or academic interest in the family and had just begun to study public policy generally. Early interest in a global family policy waned in favor of issue-specific analyses of an increasingly sophisticated nature. Early interest in the political community began in the Johnson administration and progressed steadily to formal action in the Carter administration. Specific initiatives have recently been mounted in the religious community, and coalitions of strongly religious political activists have made their debut. Through the advent of practices such as flexitime, the business sector is increasingly exhibiting family sensitivity. The 1980 White House Conference on Families provided a common forum for all of the above, crystallizing "family policy" into a publicly visible status that some proclaim as the dominant issue of the 1980s. Since polarization of the policy actors on several issues, such as abortion, is so intense that aggressive rather than reactive stances are being taken, there is a substantial likelihood that that proclamation will be fulfilled.

At the present time, therefore, we are entering an era of explicit public policy attention to the family, which promises to be lively and, it is hoped, productive. This attention will not take place in a vacuum, however, and some larger forces that may shape its progress deserve to be discussed here.

DISCUSSION

Self-sufficiency may well be the most highly valued American trait for individuals, families, communities, and the nation as a whole. It is usually applied to individuals in a variety of ways. People pridefully refer to our tradition of rugged individualism, and the self-made man is held to be somehow superior. The quality of self-reliance is a near-synonym. Do-it-yourselfers are envied by those who aren't, and even certain types of social dropouts are viewed with respect and perhaps a little envy. Don Biggs (1973), for example, provides highly complimentary biographical sketches in his popular book about successful men and women who chucked their high-paying jobs in the pressurized "establishment" for simpler life-styles that gave them more control over the life experience; members of the back-to-the-earth movement tickled the fantasies of the disillusioned who were not quite ready to go that far. Dependency, self-sufficiency's antonym, has been continuously valued negatively in all of its forms from the level of individuals to the level of nations.

In one of psychology's most famous essays, Maslow (1943) posed a hierarchy of human needs in which the lower ones must be satisfied before the higher ones may be pursued:

Physiological needs	lower
Safety and security	
Love and belongingness	
Self-esteem	
Self-actualization	higher

Although one may quarrel with his gradations, it seems somewhat self-evident that there is some prioritization of need among individuals, families, and so on to the nation as a whole. It seems logical to assume that self-sufficiency is a better means of meeting those needs than dependency; depending on OPEC to satisfy our energy needs has produced security crises of such magnitude that a new policy goal of energy self-sufficiency was set. It seems to follow that any policy or set of policies that induces dependency rather than self-sufficiency will be short-lived, or at least should be.

It is postulated here for the sake of discussion that more and more families are concluding that they have insufficient control over the means of being self-sufficient for satisfying their collective needs. It is further postulated that people have an ideal of an "elective environment" for need satisfaction—an environment that leaves the initiative for need satisfaction with them. Such an environment includes job opportunities for income, parks for recreation, services for solving problems, housing to purchase, laws to protect their rights, and so on. Some of these environmental elements are there courtesy of the free enterprise system (jobs, housing) and some are there by governmental action (parks, services) that they, as taxpayers and voters, theoretically control.

Experience has fallen far short of the ideal. The jobs are not there for many. The bank pockets a sizeable part of the family's lifetime earnings for a rather modest house. Many government programs are far from "elective," involving elaborate application procedures to see if you "qualify," waiting lists, periodic shutdowns resulting from budget cutbacks, and frequently a take-it-or-leave-it attitude. Programs come and go as administrations change and priorities shift. Pot holes in the road are filled in *after* you destroy your front end alignment. What is needed in the environment to satisfy basic needs frequently is not there or involves a harrowing experience to access.

Responses have been predictable. Angry and frustrated people are taking to the courts in unprecedented numbers to *make* that "idiotic" system operate rationally. Cynicism seems rather widespread. Some political leaders are elected to shut down the system except for national defense and a few other necessities. And since the rules of the game seem so unfair, many feel no moral qualms about "gaming" the system for maximum personal gain; withholding information to establish eligibility for a service or avoiding taxes is common; a young acquaintance of mine freely admits he likes to find jobs that will lay him off in a few months so that he can get unemployment insurance, still working on the side and paying no taxes.

Most, however, seem to experience conflict. Only the "government" can solve problems such as inflation; bad as it is in the eyes of many, a welfare program for the poor is needed; there has to be *some* sort of a minimum wage, but the kids can't find work. A government role is seen as necessary, but "they" shouldn't botch up so much, and the total price tag for it all is getting out of hand. Those folks in Washington don't know what it's like to get an $8000 bill for Susie's treatment in the psychiatric hospital, but they'll take in hordes of refugees. So people and government are in conflict.

If one were to hire a public relations expert to project a positive image of federal family-relevant programs to the public, he would do well to project two themes. First, government is making available to people the means whereby they can satisfy their needs—jobfullness, parks for recreation, a sound free-enterprise system regulated against abuses, various professional services; in short, an elective environment. Second, the government is forming a division of labor with families to control those things beyond total individual control—inflation, drug flow, discrimination, care of the disabled, and so on. Together the image is that of a society that respects and rewards individual initiative and that takes collective action on matters for which only collective action is feasible.

Instead, a very different image is projected. Regulations are seen as tying the private sector's hands so that prices rise. There are more incentives for getting on welfare than off. The courts decide whether your daughter can get an abortion. The programs are so loosely run that even doctors rip off programs such as Medicaid and Medicare. Your taxes go up if you marry the person you're living with. Drugs flow into Miami like water; they are consumed openly in the schools, and if your acting-out, drug-dependent teenager gets hauled into court, they take it out on *you*. Hardly a positive image.

Yet, realistically, all government programs are not that bad and one wonders why so many people regard government almost as an alien, subversive force. Perhaps some of the negative thinking reflects officialdom's preoccupation with pathology. Courses in growth and development, judging from an inspection of the available texts, tend to be courses in *abnormal* growth and development. We describe the health of the population in terms of *mortality* rates rather than survival rates. Even when progress is made, we talk about a decline in job*less*ness rather than an increase in job*full*ness. There is no simple term for the opposite of divorce rate. What is the antonymn for urban blight? Even research instruments accentuate the negative. Sociologists use an "alienation" scale—what's the antonym for alienation?—that has four subscales that read like the four horsemen of the Apocalypse: social isolation, powerlessness, normlessness, and meaninglessness. Throughout these pages I have used the term control as the opposite of powerlessness; why isn't the scale called "sense of control" rather than powerlessness? And what findings does one expect when the powerlessness scale includes response items such as: "There's very little that persons like me can do to improve world opinion of the United States." Wouldn't focusing questions on things that are realistically more controllable provide a more valuable insight into what people really think they can control?

The truth of the matter is that the professional world is oriented to pathology rather than normalcy, to treatment and rehabilitation rather than to prevention and especially promotion. Policies that focus on treatment and rehabilitation expand the role of the professional in the service system; policies that focus on prevention and promotion support the family's efforts on its own behalf. The locus of control shifts from consumer to provider when one focuses on pathology rather than normalization.

Is the family the problem or the solution? If it is the problem, we need to expand our treatment service systems; if it is the solution, we need to support its efforts to be self-sufficient in satisfying its needs—not only for safety and security and problem solving, but for self-actualization. If it is both, we need a balanced mixed strategy.

All of the above is theoretical, of course, and the unfortunate reality is that it does not translate readily into action. "Promoting" healthy families runs immediately into the difficulty of defining what a healthy family is. Indeed, since we are blessed with a pluralistic society with pluralistic family life-styles, what are the characteristics of health of each? What does each type of family need to control to meet its needs?

Specific, widely applicable, major strategies for promotion and prevention are few in number. Certainly inflation control, jobfullness, discrimination control, and interest rate control are starters, but it does not appear that we have the capability of formulating a detailed "family promotion" policy. We do have the capability of expanding our treatment and rehabilitation programs. Yet, expanding just those programs is Bower's bucket—ladling out without turning off the tap. And the very process of expanding just those programs is somewhat counterproductive since the rising tax burden and/or the rising inflation from deficit spending constrains the economic flexibility of the very families whose health and well-being we would prefer to be promoting. An unfortunate dilemma.

The contribution of the professional to the policy process is largely driven by the ethic of the "technological imperative"—a term framed by a long "disremembered" author. This ethic simply holds that we *should* do what we *can* do. Technological capability cannot ethically be withheld from those who can benefit from it. Unfortunately, technological capacity is not balanced. Our capabilities for promotion and prevention are far less developed than for treatment and rehabilitation, and public policies that cumulatively reflect this imbalance are counterproductive in two ways. First, as stated above, a "treatment"-dominated system constitutes a Bower's bucket syndrome. Public health thinking is particularly clear about this; if you have a polluted water supply, treating today's dysentery cases will not reduce the number of new cases tomorrow—treatment proceeds indefinitely; surgically treating lung cancer cases today will not reduce tomorrow's caseload if smoking habits go unaltered; with few exceptions, the treatment approach is, *by itself,* self-perpetuating.

Second, the treatment approach, by itself, may sometimes encourage progressive dependency rather than progressive self-sufficiency—the large tracts of the urban poor serve as a good example. The litany of government programs in such urban areas is long and dominated by the treatment approach. Instead of building a stronger society from which the massive programs can gradually be withdrawn, the programs have become the *strength* of the urban poverty society in which benefits are accessed by presenting problems; a counterproductive phenomenon. (It operates almost exactly the same way as when middle class people stay in jobs they despise for the benefits: they have too much into the retirement system and too much pay-rewarded seniority to get out constructively. Welfare recipients intensely dislike the system, but making the transition out permanently is so risky that it may not be in their best interest to try; their lives are networked into the system's benefits and many of their life-skills are in gaming it for maximum gain—a sound economic strategy.)

At first blush, the task at hand is to immediately improve our technological capabilities for promotion and prevention to develop a public policy front with a rational balance of promotion, prevention, treatment, and rehabilitation. Yet the need to respect self-determination makes that difficult for some preventive and promotional activities. If, for instance, the high proportion of female-headed households in need of government support programs inclines policymakers to offer incentives for other types of family life-styles, those incentives are discriminatory against those female-headed families that are happy and stable and wouldn't have it any other way. Early in professional training, the neophyte is instructed in not superimposing his values on his patients or on society; this is even more binding for government officials who cannot favor one form of legal life-style over another.

Part of the answer (or the problem) may lie in the division of labor between the public and private sectors. The public official who weaves his personal values into public policy will be severely chastised, but if his twin does the same thing successfully in the private sector, he is called a leader. Advocates of life-styles that lead to a full life and that minimize the risk of pathology are in short supply, and if the public sector moves more quickly with a treatment/rehabilitation agenda than the private sector moves with a promotion/prevention agenda, the expensive counterproductivities noted above will result. Another dilemma.

The "apple pie and motherhood" reception to the early idea of family policy ages quickly when the complexities of the effort are considered. No easy solutions are readily apparent and analyses on the full scale of the problem are still primitive. Indeed, one may question whether we are ready for family policy. The early readiness to adopt a global family policy has been rejected by most in favor of a piecemeal approach to the problem, which seems to be a prime example of the technological imperative. "One global family policy is useless now. All I know is that we can improve AFDC benefits here and improve child care for migrant families there and put in group homes for the retarded somewhere else. These are things we can do now, so let's get on with it." The appeal of this contemporary logic is diluted when one considers that the cumulative impact of these implemented capabilities may be so overweighted in treatment approaches that, in the year 2000, we still have the same magnitude of problems plus more government dependency.

The opinion here, therefore, is that neither extreme is desirable—neither the harmless global policy nor the current preference for the fractional approach.

Yet the climate is ripe for action now and the notion of control seems paramount for guiding initial steps. Although families are clamoring for more control over their lives, they are not exercising the controls they now have. If people voluntarily controlled their tobacco/drug/alcohol use, the preventive benefits to families would be enormous. Government efforts to assist families with their control efforts deserve top priority as an entire class of actions. (A new journal, *Family and Community Health,* was founded on just that philosophy.) Additionally, government is not exercising all of its preventive controls. Improved levels of jobfullness, interest rates, and inflation rates are some of many attainable goals. The cost of the two levels of preventive control strategies is large, but it is a testable and probably supportable hypothesis that such a preventive policy strategy is the most economic alternative technologically attainable that is appropriate for government and that is consistent with the public's expectations. Treatment policies will always be needed, but the magnitude of need simply must be reduced to affordable proportions. Such a purposeful approach would not be a cure-all (or a prevent-all), but would be a significant improvement over either the global policy or the fractional policy approaches.

It is necessary at this point to interject another consideration—what is the capacity of federal government for formulating and continuously implementing a balanced family policy strategy? Experience seems to suggest that government is most efficient for categorical programs at the federal level. These programs emanate from specific pieces of legislation with a clearly circumscribed problem, with specific target populations and objectives, and with a clearly defined implementation strategy. Such a set of programs requires coordination, at which the federal government has been admittedly less efficient than desirable. In my present position I have seen several attempts to involve officials in the major categorical programs in efforts to integrate the programs into a cohesive conceptual whole, with the same result as the Tower of Babel. There are so many dimensions to public policy and people bring so many different conceptual orientations to them that broad-scale, purposeful, integrated functioning has proved to be an elusive goal.

It seems, therefore, that an opportunity and a need present themselves simultaneously. The opportunity is for immediate and continuous work on a large variety of policy options for various dimensions of the family, one by one. Political activists seem ready for this, as do members of the professional/scientific community and members of the political community, and this is what the federal bureaucracy is capable of implementing. Yet this fractional approach to policy development produces a need to evaluate the cumulative impact of all the emerging policies to assess whether the total effort constitutes an unbalanced strategy. At present this need seems poorly appreciated, and may leave the total federal system of family-relevant efforts to chance as policy management improves its capacity for systemic integration.

PROGNOSTICATIONS

It is enjoyable to engage in discussions such as the above and it is even more enjoyable to engage in some prognostications. Five are offered here.

1. A sense of history suggests that family policy is not only here to stay, but will continue to grow into a larger and more serious effort.
2. Since many of the participants in the policy process—combatants, if you prefer—hold mutually exclusive positions on issues such as abortion, the policy scene should be quite lively.
3. Initial efforts probably will proceed issue by issue, creating a future need for assessments of how balanced the total effort is.
4. Not everyone will be satisfied with the efforts in the years ahead. People differ drastically on specific issues, on the role of government relative to the family, and on the priorities that are needed to give government a balanced family strategy.
5. Progress will be very, very slow, with many a backward step.

The stakes are high, however, and it is well worth the effort for all to participate.

Epilogue

It has been six months since the preceding chapters were completed shortly after the November, 1980, elections, and a final update before publication seems in order.

Over the past few months, there has been intense press coverage of the Reagan administration's proposals for tax cuts, cutbacks in federal spending in nearly all departments except defense, conversion of various federal categorical programs to block grants to the states, elimination of some programs (e.g., CETA, an employment program) and reduction in others (e.g., Food Stamps), and a general reduction in the federal work force. Although most of these are still in the proposal stage awaiting Congressional action, it is quite clear that we are experiencing a revolution of long-lasting proportions. Large numbers of people, in contrast to recent years, will not directly benefit from federally supported programs; training and research programs will be severely affected; and there will be a shift of responsibility to state government.

All of this has been well publicized, of course, and most policy analysts ascribe these changes to the Reagan administration. A few policy analysts, however, especially economists, take a longer view and maintain that changes of this type were inevitable and actually began in the Carter administration. Such analysts see federal public welfare expenditures as a function of prevailing economic conditions, in which the economy serves as the moon and public welfare expenditures as the tide.

Robert Harris is one such analyst who presented his views at an HHS-sponsored Social Services Policy Conference in Washington approximately one month after the election and *before* the Reagan proposals were publicly articulated in detail.

Harris, an Urban Institute policy analyst at the time, began his historical analysis in 1950, stating that 9% of the GNP (gross national product) was spent that year on public welfare programs (PWP). This increased to 12% in 1966 and 20% in 1975, declining slightly since then. The 1950–1965 period saw the increase in PWP exceed the rate of growth of the GNP, and this accelerated markedly in the 1965–1975 period.

A factor underlying this growth was the rapid expansion of the economy, especially in the 1960s, which sharply increased public revenues. If unspent, Harris maintains, those revenues would have constituted a drag on the economy, so that increased federal spending or tax cuts were necessary. Both were tried from time to time, with increased spending the more dominant of the two. Many of the resulting programs were indexed, assuring that future growth in response to inflation would be automatic.

The cumulative public debt that resulted from a cooling economy in a period of steadily increasing federal PWP spending strained the political climate to the point that President Carter withdrew his January, 1980, budget to avoid a confrontation with Congress over deficit spending. Reagan's promise to further cut deficit federal spending was a key factor in the 1980 election.

Harris maintains that anyone elected in 1980 would have been forced to curtail spending sooner or later—demographic trends will demand it. In reference to the aging of the U.S. population, Harris states:

> One recent study concluded that the elderly's share of the federal budget will rise slowly and steadily through the rest of this century, reaching 32 percent in the year 2000 from existing programs. It will then leap upward to 42 percent in 2015, and soar to 63 percent by 2025, again *without any new programs*. This growth, in my view, will not be permitted to happen.

Thus, it appears that we are entering a public policy era in which the principal question is, *How much can we afford, irrespective of desires and even need?* Additionally, with a fixed level of public expenditures, *How will priorities be set?* Finally, *How formally will family well-being be considered in the priority-setting process?*

Most policy analysts agree that short run efforts to strengthen the economy will benefit middle and upper income families at the expense of lower income families which are the direct beneficiaries of government programs. No consensus exists on the long run effects, largely because it is not clear at this writing how many of the Reagan proposals will receive sustained Congressional support. No analyst known to me, however, sees a return to the spending sprees of the 1960s at any time in the foreseeable future. It is difficult to avoid concluding that the blossoming of interest in family public policy has been poorly timed, indeed.

Meanwhile, the implementation phase of the White House Conference on Families ended on March 31, 1981, without fanfare, and the future of the new (still understaffed) Office for Families is questionable. Interestingly, the key actors in the 1980 White House Conference on Families, pro and con, seem undaunted at the moment, with many already relocated in new positions in both public and private sectors. It will be fascinating to watch the nation's family policy leaders reorganize and reorient themselves over the remainder of the 1980s.

Describing the current state of family public policy has been likened to changing one of your car's tires while you drive down the highway at 55 mph. Rapid change is the order of the day, and it is expected to be so indefinitely.

For reasons that should be self-evident, I am reminded at this moment of a conclusion attributed to two Scottish scholars twenty years ago who had just lost their research grant: "Bruce, we're out of money—now we've got to think."

Appendix

The Sixty Recommendations from the White House Conference on Families

(Recommendations from all three White House Conferences on Families are in the WHCF's final report: *Listening to America's families: Action for the 80s* (October, 1980).)

The 60 Baltimore WHCF recommendations were clustered into the following four topics:

Families and economic well-being
Families: challenges and responsibilities
Families and human needs
Families and major institutions

Votes for each recommendation were on a scale of strongly agree/moderately agree/moderately disagree/strongly disagree.

The 60 recommendations are provided below, clustered into the four topic areas. Following this listing of recommendations is the official vote tally chart, which provides the rank of each recommendation among all 60 recommendations, the rank of each recommendation in its topic area, the total yes votes (strongly agree + moderately agree), the total no votes (moderately disagree + strongly disagree), and the number of votes by degree of agreement.

FAMILIES AND ECONOMIC WELL-BEING

Economic Pressures

1. It is imperative that all branches of government strengthen and enforce existing legislation on programs of full employment. Each person should have the opportunity to obtain a job which provides a feeling of usefulness and dignity at wages sufficient to support a decent standard of living.

    The Humphrey-Hawkins Act must be implemented—not ignored. Teenagers, minorities, women, all unemployed and under-employed must have specifically targeted programs, initiated and carried out by government and industry to assure full employment.

2. Since inflation is one of the most destructive elements affecting families, we move that government anti-inflation policies should place special emphasis on components that hit families hardest; food, health, energy and housing.

   Federal, State and local governments should support a coherent energy program (including all energy sources, and support for mass transit), comprehensive national health program, and lower interest rates to enable families to buy homes and to meet other family needs. Anti-inflation programs should not be at the expense of human services such as employment, housing and welfare. Government should refrain from policies that cause unemployment in order to slow the economy and control inflation.

3. Federal, State and local governments should take positive steps to improve the employment situation by:

   ▶The vigorous enforcement of existing legislation prohibiting racial, sexual and age discrimination in employment, such as the Civil Rights Act, Age Discrimination in Employment Act and other affirmative action programs;

   ▶The establishment of special services in the Small Business Administration for the encouragement and financing of family enterprises, and;

   ▶The participation of the development of comprehensive skill training centers under adult education programs for family members who are unemployed or under-employed; providing adequate financial support to families attending such centers.

Family and Work

4. Full employment is essential to the economic and general well-being of families. It can be assisted through government policy, such as enunciated in the Humphrey-Hawkins Act. Citizen groups and government agencies should monitor effective enforcement of these policies. Career counseling, career development, vocational education, and personnel manpower training especially targeted at the unemployed or under-employed need to be redirected and expanded to reflect current needs and expected developments in employment. This should be done through cooperative efforts of industry, labor, community groups and government. Adequate public transportation to connect rural and city people with job markets should be addressed.

5. Business, labor and government should encourage and implement employment opportunities and personnel policies that enable persons to hold jobs while maintaining a strong family life. Family-oriented personnel policies can result in reduced absenteeism, greater productivity and decreased stress. Toward such desirable ends there is need for creative development of such work arrangements as flextime, flexible leave policies for both sexes, job sharing programs, dependent care options and part-time jobs with pro-rated pay and benefits. Additionally, employers should recognize the possible adverse effects of relocation on families so that they may provide support and options.

6. We urge: effective monitoring and implementation of laws concerning fair employment practice in accordance with legislative intent, emphasizing improved enforcement procedures against discrimination in employment (based on race, color, national origin, sex, age, religion, and disability) such as—affirmative action, equal pay for equal work, employee development and promotion, and prohibition of sexual harrassment; that federal, state and local governments be urged to explore ways to define and support equal pay for comparable work. We urge the White House and states to do everything possible to ensure ratification of ERA.

Tax Policies

7. President and Congress should encourage family responsibilities and functions through:
   ▶additional first year exemption for birth or adoption of a child
   ▶double day care credit for handicapped or elderly dependent without existing taxpayer work requirement
   ▶$250 credit for elderly dependents in taxpayer's home
   ▶expand Earned Income Tax Credit to benefit families with children up to the BLS (Bureau of Labor Statistics) lower living standard
   ▶deductions for Family Responsibility Savings Accounts for:
   •dependent education
   •handicapped dependent care
   •first home purchase
   •retirement of family members regardless of work history
   •increased day care credit from 20 to 35%
   •refundable day care credit

8. We recommend that the President propose and/or the Congress enact legislation to provide for the equitable taxation of two-worker married couples through the elimination of the marriage penalty by permitting married individuals the option of using the tax rate for single individuals.

9. We recommend that the President propose and/or the Congress enact legislation which would adjust the federal personal income tax rates and brackets to avoid the inflation penalty. With the current level of inflation and high prospects of a long-term inflation trend, this adjustment must be substantial. Such action would also correct the unlegislated increase in tax burden on families.

Income Security for Families

10. The Federal Government shall ensure a minimum living standard for all citizens in the United States and territories. The AFDC and UP programs shall be combined into a Family Assistance program, providing 100% of the lower level standard of living, regionally adjusted, fully funded by the Federal Government. Child Support Laws apply to either or both parents. Federal income tax refund set aside programs shall be a means of enforcing child support laws, and state compliance incentives shall be provided by the Federal Government. All providers under investigation for fraud participating in income assistance programs shall have a stay placed on bank accounts.

11. We recommend Social Security allow:
    ▶Higher limits on income earned in retirement.
    ▶Removal of dependency category for spouses and development of an earned sharing program providing coverage for both spouses based on 50/50 distribution of combined credits during marriage, dispersed at divorce or retirement.
    ▶Providing quarters of men and women's coverage for child-rearing time taken off from employment.
    ▶Handicapped and elderly to live at home with reimbursable services given now by hospitals and nursing homes; and extended time for services in hospitals and homes.
    ▶SSI to have non-discriminatory eligibility definitions.
    ▶Survivor benefits to be given regardless of age and children.

12. Full employment opportunity should be supported by the Government through the private and public sector toward the support of self-sufficiency and short-term total government dependency. Appropriate preventive–comprehensive sup-

portive services ought to be available including appropriate access services enhancing upward mobility, such as transportation, childcare, etc. The provision of supportive services should be non-punitive and should build on strengths in the family and other voluntary and informal support systems and should be achieved through a partnership arrangement between the public and voluntary and non-profit sector.

Status of Homemakers

13. The intrinsic value of homemakers should have national recognition as a conceptual and practical framework for legal parents/guardians performing a primary nurturing, socializing responsibility within the family unit. Action: Promote positive recognition and active support of the primary homemaker, through:
    ▶Public awareness initiatives that declare the intrinsic value of the homemaker.
    •media campaigns
    •education
    •establishment of homemaking as a career by the Department of Labor
    •government declaration which prescribes an established time such as National Homemakers Week for recognition of primary homemaker.
14. Local, state, and federal governments should recognize the economic and career value of homemaking. Marriage is also an economic partnership and financial resources earned by the spouses should be shared equally. Social security and pension funds should be vested equally during marriage without reducing existing benefits. Assets accrued during marriage should be considered equally earned and owned so that at dissolution it can be divided fairly or at death there is no tax when passed on to the surviving husband or wife. Assistance to displaced homemakers, particularly in job training, can be supplied by the public and private sectors.
15. Revise IRS laws to provide:
    ▶additional tax exemption for homemakers providing primary care for preschool, handicapped, and/or elderly family members in the home;
    ▶eliminate inheritance tax for spouses.

FAMILIES: CHALLENGES AND RESPONSIBILITIES

Preparation for Marriage and Family Life

16. Federal, state and local governments support development, personnel training and implementation through public/private sectors of comprehensive bilingual, multicultural family life education for children, youth and adults. Parents, children, youth and community representatives (teachers, clergy and family professionals), shall plan, implement, and evaluate experiential and didactic programs. They should be holistic, recognizing ethnical and personal dimensions of human sexuality, respecting all sectarian positions and including parenting education, communication and decision-making skills, law, interpersonal relationships, medical and natural family planning and sex roles. Community organizations, businesses and other family-serving groups share responsibility for family life education.
17. Recognizing that many marriages are already in serious trouble within the first 18 months, we recommend that tax incentives be given to couples participating in public or private experimental programs exploring responsibilities of marriage

before and up to 18 months after the marriage. In addition, marriage and family counseling should be recognized and actively supported by both government and non-government agencies as both preventive and treatment approaches to help strengthen families.

18. It is recommended that the national Government consider establishment of a publicly supported center for the study of prevention. This center would serve as a clearinghouse for the development and publicizing of information about effective practices and models which prevent family conflict, child abuse, spouse abuse, neglect, emotional disturbance, and other forms of personal and family dysfunction. Costly rehabilitative and treatment programs will continue to grow unless increased study and funding is devoted to preventive approaches which promote wholesome personal and family health.

Studies undertaken would require normal informed consent of participants and parents for minor children.

Specific Supports and Families

19. The White House Conference on families recommends that government and the private sector join together to provide supports to meet the special needs of families. Federally-supported programs should encourage agencies and organizations to seek ways to involve families in the provision of services. Federally-supported programs should provide incentives for linkages with public, private, multi-cultural community-based systems, and voluntary organizations. Services should include the use of volunteers and family self-help programs. We further recommend that federal and other support programs designed to help families offer services to the entire family as well as the individual.

20. Recognizing that family stability is a national societal strength, governmental, private, and non-profit agencies should provide family enrichment programs and develop such programs where needed. Recognizing the unique needs of all families we draw attention to:
    ▶ the nuclear and extended families and their support;
    ▶ the single parent families and their support;
    ▶ the military families and their support;
    ▶ the migrant, immigrant and dislocated families and their support.

21. Every private and public agency should be encouraged to write a family impact statement as part of every policy implemented. Legislation to this end shall be adequately provided by federal, state and local legislative bodies, that voluntary independent commissions for families be created by interested localities and states, and at the national level, to ensure that public policies impacting on families, including those of business and industry, be sensitive to the diversity of families and accountable to their special needs.

Parents and Children

22. Resolved: that WHCF recognizes that current Federal policies in foster care and adoption have unnecessarily deleterious effects on families and children and that a reorientation of these policies is long overdue; that WHCF accepts H.R. 3434 as a bill that effectively redresses many of the inequities presently in law and notes that it has broad and enthusiastic support among persons and groups advocating policy reform in these areas; that therefore, WHCF strongly endorses H.R. 3434 and calls upon Congress and the President to enact it into law forthwith.

23. Preventive approaches to the crisis of teenage pregnancy must receive high priority. These should include, but not be limited to, family life education and comprehensive health services. This may be provided by parents, religious institutions, community organizations and/or public and private agencies. Pregnant adolescents, adolescent parents and their families should have access to comprehensive health, education, and social services that will help them overcome the problems associated with early pregnancy and teenage parenthood.
24. Whereas a child without supportive and nurturing parental relationships is a hurting and damaged child; and whereas Federal, State and local programs should not alienate children psychologically or spiritually from their parents; and whereas closer ties between parents and their children is to be presumed a good—not an ill—be it resolved that parents not be excluded from decision-making participation in those programs which affect their children and youth, unless the protection of the interests and rights of the individual family member is at risk especially in the case of children and youth.

Family Violence

25. Federal, State and local governments should give a high priority to preventing and dealing with all victims of domestic violence and neglect by helping all types of families to avoid stress, violence, and crisis through allocation of more monies or reallocation of existing monies for multicultural:
    ▶treatment services, preventive services and research;
    ▶development and implementation of educational curricula and enhanced professional training in family life, parenting, sex roles, sexuality, and intergenerational relationships starting in kindergarten;
    ▶media campaigns that promote greater public awareness of, and responsibility for prevention of family stress crises and violence.
26. Federal, State and local governments should give highest priority to the development and implementation of comprehensive treatment services and programs to alleviate stress, violence and crises in all types of intimate relations and families by:
    ▶establishing family multi-service centers to provide convenient, comprehensive affordable, multi-lingual 24-hour services;
    ▶providing community crises shelters with supportive health, legal and rehabilitative services to abuse victims and their dependents including counseling, referral advocacy and community education and self-help programs;
    ▶mandating interagency coordination of services and the inclusion of community-based and advocacy groups.
27. The Federal Government must take the leadership role and responsibility through the passage and funding of the Domestic Violence Prevention and Services Act of 1980 and increased funding under the Child Abuse Act of 1974 for the research and development of services through a single coordinated federal effort. Pre-existing programs should be promoted and strengthened. Planning should come from a state agency with service delivery by community and self-help groups, providing multi-cultural/lingual programs focusing on interrelationships of family abuse. All levels of government should strictly enforce current laws, enact appropriate new laws, and provide funds for related training of criminal justice personnel.

Substance Abuse

28. As substance abuse, including alcohol, causes many severe family problems, preventive programs should include:

▶Schools, K-12, and agencies should provide educational and vocational preventive studies concerning dangers of alcohol, drug abuse, abuse of prescription drugs, and the necessity of positive parental example.

▶Media should avoid showing drugs as a cure-all, promote public awareness of constructive alternatives, and must provide equal time to counteract alcohol commercials.

▶There should be a movement toward parental meetings, both with and without children to educate them regarding prevention.

▶Medical professionals should undergo extensive training on drug abuse, especially prescription drugs and alcohol.

29. It should be the policy of government and private agencies to offer a wide range of community-based substance abuse treatment programs—that is, accessible to families and in the language and culture of these families receiving services. These treatment programs should include a multi-disciplinary team, holistic approach which encourages strong family participation and offers a variety of options, e.g. employment and student assistance programs, self-help groups, residential facilities, etc. Programs should be accountable and client follow-up done. Throughout treatment and intervention, the primary focus should be on the family.

30. Alcohol, drug abuse and nicotine abuse are our number one health problem. Society denies this problem because of its dependence on these substances. We recommend that these problems receive the highest priority. This includes no budget cuts and sufficient funding for prevention and treatment; a recognition of the cultural and economic aspects of drugs and alcohol; the need for changing attitudes; the need for family and community involvement; and the need for national efforts against the drug and alcohol epidemic. We should help children discover their gifts, talents and abilities and cultivate these through a strong, loving family to raise the children's self-esteem.

Aging and Families

31. That the Social Security (SS) System be reformed so that:

▶two independent persons receiving SS payments will experience no reduction because of marriage;

▶limitation on earned income will be eliminated for those collecting SS;

▶all assured an adequate income level;

▶all pre-retirees receive an adequate and simple explanation of SS benefits in their dominant language.

32. To encourage home care support alternatives to institutionalization and promote choice for families and the elderly, we recommend:

▶appropriate changes in Medicaid/Medicare policies;

▶tax benefits to cover costs incurred for homemaker services, day care, night care, transportation, and appropriate home improvements;

▶local development of services by the public or private sectors such as telephone reassurances, meals on wheels, friendly visiting, companionship, dial-a-ride and respite care;

▶funding services to help elderly individuals maintain their own homes.

33. To revise the tax laws to benefit families who care for and keep the elderly in their own homes which provides a tax incentive for a household that includes a person 65 years of age or older. Should that household modify its dwelling to accommodate an older person, an additional tax incentive should be given and we recommend that public policy provide tax incentives to individuals who assist

older citizens without regard to income qualifications and study the effect of how family support is considered in determination of income eligibility for the elderly to participate in programs.

FAMILIES AND HUMAN NEEDS

Education

34. Priority should be given to Family Life Education through all life cycles (K-12, Continuing Education, Higher Education, Vocational Education, Community Education) which includes:
    ▶parenting skills
    ▶communication skills
    ▶life skills (effective use of family resources be encouraged through education in: consumer homemaking, budgeting and money management, nutrition, energy, family health, use of time and other related home management and home maintenance skills).

35. Federal government should increase its funding of education. Congress should increase appropriations to implement the federally mandated programs. Priority should be given to increasing state and local appropriations and standards for quality sex-equitable educational programs inclusive of:
    ▶K-12
    ▶Bilingual Education
    ▶Special Education (Including Exceptional and Gifted)
    ▶Community Education
    ▶Education for Handicapped Persons
    ▶Continuing Education
    ▶Vocational Education
    ▶Adult Education
    ▶Higher Education

36. Public education must be maintained. The federal and state governments should work to secure equal educational opportunity for every child. This education should recognize the multi-ethnic diversity of our nation.

    Children must be taught in language they understand. Bi-lingual, bi-cultural programs which reflect the culture and traditions of our pluralistic society should be instituted as part of the process of learning English and becoming integrated into the mainstream of American life.

    Congress should enact legislation and appropriate adequate funds for awareness training for educators in order to deal more effectively with the diversified needs of students.

Health

37. Comprehensive health care should be totally accessible to all segments of the community, recognizing that special emphasis must be directed toward the medically underserved families in rural and urban locations. Specifically, access barriers such as culture, geography, physical barriers and cost must be adequately addressed, if this goal is to be achieved. The WHCF should support and encourage the continued use of medically underserved areas, health manpower shortage areas, and health underserved rural areas as the criteria for establishing priorities when distributing federal funds.

38. Whereas families are responsible for the prevention of disease and the promotion of wellness, in both the physical and mental health of their members: We urge that the private and public sectors focus their resources toward prevention, voluntary early intervention, education, and outreach services, in both specific and comprehensive programs. These should be both accessible for all segments of the community and reimbursed by third party payors or tax credits. Priority shall be to eliminate the discrepancy in health status between the minority and general populations and reduce suicide, homicide, alcohol and drug related deaths.

39. America was founded on deeply held principles of religious freedom, liberty and pluralism.

    The decision whether to have a child is a personal decision of conscience for each woman in consultation with a doctor.

    Government restrictions would endanger the health and well-being of the woman and the family. Therefore, the full range of family planning services including pre- and post-natal care and safe, legal abortion must be available to all who freely make this decision.

    Regarding abortion and all reproductive services, neither the WHCF nor the government should pass any proposal that should be mandatory for parent or child.

Housing

40. We recommend that the federal government, states and localities assure the right of all families to safe, decent, affordable and energy-efficient housing.

    A. Implement legislation and additional appropriations to increasing low and moderate cost housing available for rental, home and apartment ownership, including:
    ▶Additional tax incentives to homeowners, housing providers and lenders.
    ▶Subsidies for low-interest loans for homeowners.
    ▶Acknowledgment of "sweat equity" (to increase loan *amounts* available to homeowners).
    ▶Expansion of "Homesteading" Programs.
    ▶Real Property tax abatement for homeowners.
    ▶Rental and mortgage payment subsidies.
    ▶Tax-free housing revenue bonds.

    B. Citizen participation planning, implementation and monitoring be mandated.

41. We recommend that all discriminatory practices in housing against any family regardless of size or composition be prohibited at all levels of government. This policy should be implemented by:
    ▶Strict *enforcement* of existing legislation.
    ▶Enactment of Edwards-Drinan Bill (Enforcement of Title VIII "Fair Housing Act" by H.U.D.).
    ▶Enact legislation for the public and private sector prohibiting discrimination against families with children, aged, handicapped and singles.
    ▶State enactment of "Fair-Share" housing laws.

42. We recommend that state and local governments shall recognize the interdependence of our current programs in order to promote the coordination among health, education, social welfare, transportation, child care, energy and environmental programs to assure the preservation of a sense of neighborhood (1) through the encouragement of home ownership and effective rehabilitation (2) through the development of effective housing codes and code enforcement at

state and local levels to prevent the displacement of families due to lack of repair and maintenance by landlords, the lack of protection for renters in buildings subject to condominium conversion and tax delinquency.

Child Care

43. That federal, state and local government and private industry redirect and expand current funding for quality child care to provide family support and preventive services for all families who require these services including, but not limited to, child care services that would prevent the removal of children from their own homes and into institutions and foster care settings.
44. In order to assure that child care programs involve families and reflect their diverse values and choices for their children, it should be the policy of government at all levels to promote the development of alternative forms of quality care, both center and home based. Families must be central to any child care program for ideal impact on children's development.
45. To ensure the safety, health and developmental potential of children, quality licensing standards for all child care programs should be required on the local, state, and federal levels and these standards should require that child care personnel be adequately trained and receive wages which fit the level of qualifications and competencies required.

Handicapping Conditions

46. To assist families with disabled members to live productive, independent lives within the community, emphasis should be placed on respite care; attendant care; subsidized adoption with medical assistance; early identification; diagnosis and infant stimulation programs, financial assistance for special equipment of the working and nonworking disabled, the design of adaptive products by industry, employment opportunities to encourage self-support, tax deductions to encourage families to care for disabled members of all ages at home, counseling, low-interest mortgage loans and assistance in adapting homes to meet individual needs and full implementation and funding existing laws and programs.
47. Educate the public and private sectors to the value of handicapped persons in our society to achieve total integration.
    ►education of employers and employees to capabilities and needs of handicapped persons within work force;
    ►appropriate training of handicapped persons for career, home and life skills;
    ►organizations and institutions build into their professional school curricula standards for accreditation, in-service training, the appropriate educational information and requirements to create a responsive service delivery system;
    ►use of handicapped persons to promote national media campaign to educate the public; and,
    ►secondary educational curricula include practical work with handicapped persons.
48. Government at all levels must develop and implement policies and programs responsive to the needs of handicapped persons and their families.
    ►Tax credits for families caring for handicapped persons; i.e., housing, equipment, personal care, adoption.
    ►To finance and implement present and future laws which are supportive; i.e., transportation, fair housing, income maintenance, education, mortgage guarantees, adoption, advocacy, rehabilitation.

▶Provide option to institutionalization; i.e., community alternative living arrangements, respite care, homemaker services, parental counseling, training, day programming recreation.

▶Insurance and licensing discrimination should be eliminated.

▶Cut red tape and bureaucracy to encourage the support of the private sector.

FAMILIES AND MAJOR INSTITUTIONS

Government

49. We support policies which preserve and protect basic legal and human rights of all family members. To guarantee these rights we support:

▶Ratification of the ERA.

▶Elimination of discrimination and encouragement of respect for differences based on sex, race, ethnic origin, creed, socio-economic status, age, disability, diversity of family type and size, sexual preference or biological ties.

▶Protection against violent and abusive action.

▶Right to open, accessible, accountable, and responsive government at all levels.

▶Right to decide whether or not to bear a child including access to the full range of family planning services, abortion, and maternal and infant care.

50. (Family Impact Analysis) structures representative of the diversity of family life should be established by state and local constituencies to provide a voice for families, family impact studies and family research programs. At the federal level, accountability should be implemented through the establishment of an independent high level cross cutting commission to monitor and evaluate the impact of federal policies on families.

More organizations and agencies—both public and private—should examine and improve the ways in which their own practices affect families.

51. (Resolve) that government assume responsibility for enhancing the ability of families to function by guaranteeing basic human needs necessary for their material, physical, intellectual and emotional development, with the objective of providing for the independence and self sufficiency of families. Such basic needs include universal health insurance, jobs which enhance dignity and respect, guaranteed adequate income, safe and decent housing, and access to education and day care and that government regulations, governing aid to families with dependent children programs, or those on public assistance, be changed to eliminate disincentives to a father staying in the household to support his family so that the family can begin functioning as an economic unit.

Media

52. The FCC should require stations to fully inform the public in prime time as to the ways they can effectively respond to objectionable material and further that the FCC should establish a grievance mechanism at regional levels to address complaints or objections in addition to seeking a commission membership which is reflective of cultural and ethnic diversity and increases the positive visibility of ethnic and racial minorities. To ensure more general involvement in the station's programming, commercial stations should be required to form community Advisory Boards before license renewal, as they are now required for public broadcasting systems.

53. Families, community groups and the general public should marshall their forces to persuade advertising sponsors, government agencies and the media to eliminate the violence and the abusive programming having negative effects on the family. Any race, religious and sex stereotyping should be eliminated. Families should be educated about how to express their reactions to detrimental programming as well as the programs they endorse. Families should have the opportunity to invite mass media into their homes as safely as they invite family and friends.

54. All media must present views in a balanced manner on all issues of concern. American families rest on a foundation of diversity. Such diversity is sorely lacking in the models provided by the mass media both in advertising and in the content of entertainment fare, much of which ridicules strong family relations and provides negative roles for children and other family members. Stereotyped portrayals of women and minorities are particularly destructive and dangerous.

Community Institutions

55. That governments (1) increase support of local community organization of proven effectiveness for planning, coordination, and delivery of community services thus promoting citizen participation and self-reliance among families and strengthening institutions, such as religious groups and institutions, family law services, comprehensive health and community centers, family counseling, and community-based education centers, (2) encourage and promote the increased use of existing physical and human resources in local communities, including self-help groups, supported by a wider range of professionals, who emphasize preventive health education, (3) recognize and affirm the role of religious institutions in strengthening families and (4) provide for comprehensive, universally accessible social services.

56. In heartfelt concern that families continue to be able to choose to have children despite the present economic realities that force most parents to work, we urge community institutions to provide and support programs of maternal and paternal leave and adequate child-care options. We also urge communities to provide and support access to legal, medical help in family planning services for people of all economic circumstances to safeguard their health and their choice to have children.

57. That Governments confront the negative impact of racism and discrimination on the total community and promulgate and enforce policies that directly reduce its influence in everyday life of families. Basic social policies should ensure equity and social justice for all individuals regardless of and respecting differences of age, sex, race, ethnic, religious, cultural, or moral tradition and values. Also that community institutions have a responsibility to provide services to all members of the community and make available a choice of public and community services which take into account individual preference and differences in family makeup, and community pluralism.

Law and the Judicial System

58. It is the recommendation of the WHCF that states be encouraged to revise their justice systems to minimize disruption on families, to remove status offenders from the court structure and to consider particularly the impact which removal of children has upon families. State laws must assure that children be provided with due process protection including the hearings and legal representation and including least restrictive placement whenever they are removed from home, whether

for reasons of delinquency, dependency, mental illness, mental retardation or other social reasons. The cultural and linguistic heritage of the families involved in this process must be taken into consideration.

59. Recommend that court-connected conciliation and mediation services become available in all States and territories, with careful consideration of the linguistic and cultural difference of the involved families to assist families in self-determining issues relating to marriage, divorce, custody, support, visitation and any matter relating to their family unit; and to that end joint custody of children should, whenever possible, be preserved between the parents as an alternative mechanism to the traditional adversary system; and that the States consider laws that impact on the preservation of the family unit.

60. It is the recommendation of the WHCF that each State establish a court system or level of judiciary to deal only with legal matters affecting the family (divorce, property division, custody, support, visitation, adoption, child abuse and neglect, and other juvenile matters) and that each provide opportunities for continuing legal education and cultural awareness for the judges and attorneys serving in this capacity. Also that community advisory groups be established to assist the court in determining effectiveness of policies on family and community life. These groups should consist of parents, public and private service providers, religious interest groups and elected officials.

Recommendation Vote Tally Chart

Recomm. #	Rank overall (1–60)	Total yes	Total no	Strongly agree	Moderately agree	Moderately disagree	Strongly disagree	Rank in this topic
# 1	35	507	83	392	115	43	40	10
# 2	48	457	132	323	134	65	67	12
# 3	14	540	49	429	111	26	23	6
# 4	29	523	60	417	106	27	33	8
# 5	3	569	21	516	53	8	13	1
# 6	45	471	119	409	62	28	91	11
# 7	55	318	268	193	125	128	140	13
# 8	4	560	24	472	88	11	13	2
# 9	56	297	286	177	120	115	171	14
#10	58	283	298	164	119	122	176	15
#11	16	536	48	378	158	19	29	7
#12	32	520	59	373	147	31	28	9
#13	6	557	29	474	83	13	16	4
#14	9	549	35	454	95	21	14	5
#15	5	558	26	470	88	16	10	3
#16	40	488	106	376	112	42	64	14
#17	59	238	357	139	99	127	230	18
#18	52	418	174	273	145	88	86	16
#19	19	534	54	378	156	29	25	8
#20	50	429	168	303	126	87	81	15
#21	25	526	69	386	140	37	32	11
#22	17	535	37	461	74	18	19	7
#23	24	527	63	447	80	18	45	10

(continued)

Recommendation Vote Tally Chart (*Continued*)

Recomm. #	Rank overall (1–60)	Total yes	Total no	Strongly agree	Moderately agree	Moderately disagree	Strongly disagree	Rank in this topic
#24	54	342	252	239	103	98	154	17
#25	33	520	74	389	131	34	40	12
#26	34	513	74	379	134	33	41	13
#27	15	538	46	394	144	22	24	6
#28	1	578	15	478	100	9	6	1
#29	7	552	35	429	123	23	12	4
#30	10	547	42	439	108	29	13	5
#31	20	534	54	423	111	31	23	9
#32	2	572	22	510	62	8	14	2
#33	8	553	36	480	73	20	16	3
#34	22	531	61	432	99	22	39	6
#35	46	468	123	339	129	59	64	14
#36	42	480	114	366	114	52	62	11
#37	13	540	52	425	115	22	30	3
#38	27	524	60	402	122	30	30	9
#39	53	383	202	332	51	28	174	15
#40	43	478	102	321	157	63	39	12
#41	44	478	105	360	118	57	48	13
#42	30	523	52	364	159	31	21	10
#43	21	533	54	423	110	27	27	5
#44	11	547	44	425	122	20	24	1
#45	23	531	59	440	91	27	32	7
#46	18	534	26	436	98	19	7	4

(continued)

Recommendation Vote Tally Chart (*Continued*)

Recomm. #	Rank overall (1–60)	Total yes	Total no	Strongly agree	Moderately agree	Moderately disagree	Strongly disagree	Rank in this topic
#47	12	544	17	441	103	12	5	2
#48	26	526	33	415	111	20	13	8
#49	51	292	291	250	42	58	233	11
#50	39	492	95	352	140	53	42	6
#51	51	419	164	306	113	74	90	10
#52	41	478	91	320	158	46	45	7
#53	37	496	86	356	140	45	41	4
#54	60	218	363	132	86	128	235	12
#55	38	495	75	371	124	44	31	5
#56	47	460	114	336	124	50	64	8
#57	49	457	120	353	104	53	67	9
#58	28	523	43	406	117	18	25	1
#59	31	521	50	390	131	34	16	2
#60	36	506	60	365	141	47	13	3

Bibliography

Works that are fully referenced in the text are not included below. This applies particularly to newspaper columns, popular magazine articles, and court decisions.

Abeson, A., et al. A primer on due process: Education decisions for handicapped children. *Exceptional Children*, 1975, *42*, 68–74.

Abortion surveillance, annual summary, 1977. Washington, D.C.: Center for Disease Control, Public Health Service, USDHEW, 1979.

Abortion surveillance, annual summary, 1978. Washington, D.C.: Center for Disease Control, Public Health Service, USDHEW, 1980.

Abortions and the poor: Private morality, public responsibility. New York: The Alan Guttmacher Institute, 1979.

Ackerman, N. W. *The psychodynamics of family life*. New York: Basic Books, Inc., 1958.

American families: Trends and pressures, 1973. Hearings Before the Subcommittee on Children and Youth of the Committee on Labor and Public Welfare, United States Senate, 93rd Congress, First Session, September 24, 25 and 26, 1978. Washington, D.C.: U.S. Government Printing Office, 1974.

Aries, P. The family and the city. *Daedalus*, 1977, *106*(2), 227–237.

Authier, K. Defining the care in child care. *Social Work*, 1979, *24*(6), 500–505.

Axinn, J., & Levin, H. The family life cycle and economic security. *Social Work*, 1979, *24*(6), 540–546.

Bahr, S. J. The effects of welfare on marital stability and remarriage. *Journal of Marriage and the Family*, 1979, *41*(3), 553–559.

Barbaro, F. The case against family policy. *Social Work*, 1979, *24*(6), 455–457.

Biggs, D. *Breaking out*. New York: David McKay Company, Inc., 1973.

Blaydon, C. C., & Stack, C. B. Income support policies and the family. *Daedalus*, 1977, *106*(2), 147–161.

Boguslaw, R. *The new utopians*. Englewood Cliffs, N.J.: Prentice-Hall, Inc., 1965.

Bower, E. M. *Early identification of emotionally handicapped children in school*. Springfield, Ill.: Charles C Thomas, 1960.

Bradbury, K., et al. Public assistance, female headship, and economic well-being. *Journal of Marriage and the Family*, 1979, *41*(3), 519–535.

Brenner, H. M. Estimating social costs of national economic policy: Implications for mental and physical health, and criminal aggression. *Employment*, Vol. 1, Joint Economic Committee, Congress of the United States, 94th Congress, Second Session, October 26, 1976. Washington, D.C.: U.S. Government Printing Office, 1976.

Brieland, D. Bioethical issues in family planning. *Social Work*, 1979, *24*(6), 478–484.

Brown, L. R. *The twenty-ninth day.* New York: W. W. Norton and Company, 1978.

Burns, E. *Social security and public policy.* New York: McGraw-Hill, 1956.

Califano, J. A., Jr. *American families: Trends, pressures and recommendations.* A Preliminary Report to Governor Jimmy Carter. (Mimeo.) Washington, D.C.: U.S. Government Printing Office, September 17, 1976.

Callahan, J. J., Jr., et al. Responsibilities of families for their severely disabled elders. *Health Care Financing Review,* 1980, *1*(3), 29–48.

A call to action. United States Catholic Conference, National Conference of Catholic Bishops. Washington, D.C.: U.S. Government Printing Office, undated.

Chilman, C. S. Teenage pregnancy: A research review. *Social Work,* 1979, *24*(6), 492–498.

Clayton, R. R. The family and federal drug abuse policies–programs: Toward making the invisible family visible. *Journal of Marriage and the Family,* 1979, *41*(3), 637–647.

Cohen, N. E., & Connery, M. F. Government policy and the family. *Journal of Marriage and the Family,* 1967, *29,* 6–17.

Cohn, A. H. Effective treatment of child abuse and neglect. *Social Work,* 1979, *24*(6), 513–519.

Davis, N. Z. Ghosts, kin, and progeny: Some features of family life in early modern France. *Daedalus,* 1977, *106*(2), 87–114.

Dempsey, J. J. *Community services for retarded children: The consumer-provider relationship.* Baltimore: University Park Press, 1975.

Deniston, O. L., Rosenstock, I. M., & Gettings, V. A. Evaluation of program effectiveness. *Public Health Reports,* 1968, *83*(4), 323–335.

Downs, A. The impact of housing policies on family life in the United States since World War II. *Daedalus,* 1977, *106*(2), 163–180.

Druckman, J. M. The family-oriented policy and treatment program for female juvenile status offenders. *Journal of Marriage and the Family,* 1979, *41*(3), 627–635.

Dumon, W., & Aldous, J. European and United States political contexts for family policy research. *Journal of Marriage and the Family,* 1979, *41*(3), 497–505.

The family is basic to mental health—A proposal for an official family charter. *Family Service Highlights,* 1961, *XXII,* 31–39, 51.

Federal assistance for programs serving the handicapped. Office for Handicapped Individuals, USDHEW Pub. No. (OHDS) 79-22001. Washington, D.C.: U.S. Department of Health, Education, and Welfare, 1979.

Feldman, H. Why we need a family policy. *Journal of Marriage and the Family,* 1979, *41*(3), 453–455.

Forrest, J. D., Sullivan, E., & Tietze, C. *Abortion 1976–77: Needs and services in the United States, each state and metropolitan area.* New York: The Alan Guttmacher Institute, 1979. (a)

Forrest, J. D., Sullivan, E., & Tietze, C. Abortion in the United States, 1977–1978. *Family Planning Perspectives,* 1979, *11*(6), 329–341. (b)

Friedlander, W. A., & Apte, R. Z. *Introduction to social welfare* (Fifth ed.). Englewood Cliffs, N.J.: Prentice-Hall, Inc., 1980.

Gilbert, N. An initial agenda for family policy. *Social Work,* 1979, *24*(6), 447–450.

Glazer, N. Housing policy and the family. *Journal of Marriage and the Family,* 1967, *29*(1), 140–163.

Goddard, H. H. *The Kallikak family: A study in the heredity of feeblemindedness.* New York: Macmillan Co., 1912.

Goettee, D. Program control through systems analysis. *Perspectives in Maternal and Child Health,* 1971, *Series B,* No. 3, 1–9.

Gold, J., & Cates, W., Jr. Restriction of federal funds for abortion: 18 months later. *American Journal of Public Health,* 1979, *69*(9), 929-930.

Guillot, E. E. Congress and the family: Reflections of social processes and values in benefits in OASDI. *Social Service Review,* 1971, *45* 173-183.

Haber, L. D., & Smith, R. T. Disability and deviance: Normative adaptations of role behavior. *American Sociological Review,* 1971, *36,* 87-97.

Hareven, T. K. Family time and historical time. *Daedalus,* 1977, *106*(2), 57-70.

Hedges, J. N. Flexible schedules: Problems and issues. *Monthly Labor Review,* 1977, *100*(2), 62-65.

Henley, L. The family and the law. *The Family Coordinator,* 1977, *26*(4), 487-513.

Hill, R. L. Status of research on families. In *The status of children, youth, and families, 1979.* Administration for Children, Youth and Families, U.S. Department of Health and Human Services, DHHS Publication No. (OHDS) 80-30274. Washington, D.C.: U.S. Department of Health and Human Services, 1980.

Hofferth, S. L. Day care in the next decade: 1980-1990. *Journal of Marriage and the Family,* 1979, *41*(3), 649-657.

Jernegan, M. W. *Laboring and dependent classes in colonial America: 1607-1783.* Chicago: University of Chicago Press, 1931.

Joffe, C. Abortion work: Strains, coping strategies, policy implications. *Social Work,* 1979, *24*(6), 485-490.

Johnson, A. S., III, et al. *Toward an inventory of federal programs with direct impact on families.* Washington, D.C.: Institute for Educational Leadership, George Washington University, 1978.

Kadushin, A. *Child welfare services.* New York: Macmillan Publishing Co., Inc., 1974.

Kagan, J. The child in the family. *Daedalus,* 1977, *106*(2), 33-56.

Kamerman, S. B. *Developing a family impact statement.* New York: Foundation for Child Development, 1976.

Kamerman, S. B., & Kahn, A. J. (Eds.). *Family policy: Government and families in fourteen countries.* New York: Columbia University Press, 1978.

Kamerman, S. B., & Kahn, A. J. Comparative analysis in family policy: A case study. *Social Work,* 1979, *24*(6), 506-512.

Kanter, R. M. *Work and family in the United States: A critical review and agenda for research and policy.* New York: Russell Sage Foundation, 1977.

Langholz, B. Variable working hours in Germany. *Journal of Systems Management,* 1972, *23*(8), 30-33.

Lasch, C. *Haven in a heartless world.* New York: Basic Books, 1977.

The legal status of adolescents. San Francisco: Scientific Analysis Corporation, 1980.

Leik, R. K., & Hill, R. What price national policy for families. *Journal of Marriage and the Family,* 1979, *41*(3), 457-459.

Listening to America's families: Action for the 80s. The Report to the President, Congress and Families of the Nation, White House Conference on Families. October, 1980. Washington, D.C.: U.S. Government Printing Office.

Maslow, A. H. A theory of human motivation. *Psychological Review,* 1943, *50,* 370-396.

McDonald, G. W. Typology for family policy research. *Social Work,* 1979, *24*(6), 553-559.

Mencher, S. Social authority and the family. *Journal of Marriage and the Family,* 1967, *29*(1), 164-192.

Moen, P. Family impacts of the 1975 recession: Duration of unemployment. *Journal of Marriage and the Family,* 1979, *41*(3), 561-571.

Monk, A. Family supports in old age. *Social Work,* 1979, *24*(6), 533-538.

Morell, B. B. Deinstitutionalization: Those left behind. *Social Work,* 1979, *24*(6), 528-532.

Moroney, R. M. *The family and the state: Considerations for social policy.* London: Longman Group, Ltd., 1976.

Moroney, R. M. The issue of family policy: Do we know enough to take action? *Journal of Marriage and the Family,* 1979, *41*(3), 461-463.

Morris, R. Governmental health programs affecting the family: Some new dimensions for governmental action. *Journal of Marriage and the Family,* 1967, *29*(1), 64-70.

Mostwin, D. *Social dimensions of family treatment.* Washington, D.C.: National Association of Social Workers, 1980.

Moynihan, D. P. A family policy for the nation. *America,* 1965, *September 18,* 280-283.

Myrdal, A. *Nation and family: The Swedish experiment in democratic family and population policy.* New York: Harper and Brothers, 1941.

Nagi, S. Z. Some conceptual issues in disability and rehabilitation. In Sussman, M. B. (Ed.), *Sociology and rehabilitation.* Washington, D.C.: American Sociological Association, 1966, 100-113.

Nirje, B. The normalization principle and its human management implications. In Kugel, R., and Wolfensberger, W. (Eds.), *Changing patterns in residential services for the mentally retarded,* President's Committee on Mental Retardation, 1969, 181-195.

Nye, F. I., & McDonald, G. W. Family policy research: Emergent models and some theoretical issues. *Journal of Marriage and the Family,* 1979, *41*(3), 473-485.

Ooms, T. *Teenage pregnancy in a family context: Implications for policy.* Philadelphia: Temple University Press, in press.

Orwell, G. *Nineteen eighty-four.* New York: Harcourt-Brace, 1949.

Overcoming world hunger: The challenge ahead. Report of the Presidential Commission on World Hunger. Washington, D.C.: U.S. Government Printing Office, 1980.

Owen, J. D. Flexitime: Some problems and solutions. *Industrial and Labor Relations Review,* 1977, *30*(2), 152-160.

Padberg, W. H. Complexities of family policy: What can be done. *Social Work,* 1979, *24*(6), 451-454.

Pollak, O. The outlook for the American family. *Journal of Marriage and the Family,* 1967, *29*(1), 193-205.

Reinke, W. A. (Ed.). *Health planning: Qualitative aspects and quantitative techniques.* Baltimore: Johns Hopkins University, 1972.

Reynolds, M. C. A framework for considering some issues in special education. *Exceptional Children,* 1962, *28,* 376-380.

Roemer, M. I. Government health programs affecting the American family. *Journal of Marriage and the Family,* 1967, *29*(1), 40-63.

Rossi, A. S. A biosocial perspective on parenting. *Daedalus,* 1977, *106*(2), 1-31.

Sawhill, I. V. Economic perspectives on the family. *Daedalus,* 1977, *106*(2), 115-125.

Schorr, A. L. *Explorations in social policy.* New York: Basic Books, 1968.

Schorr, A. L. Views of family policy. *Journal of Marriage and the Family,* 1979, *41*(3), 465-467.

Schottland, C. I. Government economic programs and family life. *Journal of Marriage and the Family,* 1967, *29*(1), 71-123.

Segal, S. Community care and deinstitutionalization: A review. *Social Work,* 1979, *24*(6), 521-527.

Shostak, A. B. Education and the family. *Journal of Marriage and the Family,* 1967, *29*(1), 124-139.

Snapper, K. J. Status of families. In *The status of children, youth and families, 1979.* Administration for Children, Youth, and Families, U.S. Department of Health and Human Services, DHHS Publication No. (OHDS) 80-30274. Washington, D.C.: U.S. Department of Health and Human Services, 1980, 115-151.

Spanier, G. B., & Anderson, E. A. The impact of the legal system on adjustment to marital separation. *Journal of Marriage and the Family,* 1979, *41*(3), 605-613.

Sussman, M. B. Family. In Turner, J. B. (Ed.), *Encyclopedia of social work* (17th Ed.). Washington, D.C.: National Association of Social Workers, 1977.

Tallman, I. Implementation of a national family policy: The role of the social scientist. *Journal of Marriage and the Family,* 1979, *41*(3), 469-472.

Trader, H. P. Welfare policies and black families. *Social Work,* 1969, *24*(6), 548-552.

Vincent, C. E. Mental health and the family. *Journal of Marriage and the Family,* 1967, *29*(1), 18-39.

A vision and strategy: The plan of pastoral action for family ministry. United States Catholic Conference, National Conference of Catholic Bishops, 1978.

Wagatsuma, H. Some aspects of the contemporary Japanese family: Once Confucian, now fatherless? *Daedalus,* 1977, *106*(2), 181-210.

Wallerstein, J. S., & Kelly, J. B. Children and divorce: A review. *Social Work,* 1979, *24*(6), 468-475.

Wattenberg, E., & Reinhardt, H. Female-headed families: Trends and implications. *Social Work,* 1979, *24*(6), 460-466.

What is "mainstreaming"? *Exceptional Children,* 1975, *42,* 174.

Whiting, B. B. Changing life styles in Kenya. *Daedalus,* 1977, *106*(2), 211-225.

Wilensky, H. L., & Lebeaux, C. N. *Industrial society and social welfare.* New York: Russell Sage Foundation, 1958.

Winston, E. A national policy on the family. *Public Welfare,* 1969, January, 54-58.

Wolfensberger, W. The principle of normalization and its implications to psychiatric services. *American Journal of Psychiatry,* 1970, *127*(3), 67-73.

Woolsey, S. H. Pied piper politics and the child-care debate. *Daedalus,* 1977, *106*(2), 127-145.

Wrigley, E. A. Reflections on the history of the family. *Daedalus,* 1977, *106*(2), 71-85.

Zanker, A. When welfare states run into hard reality. *U.S. News and World Report,* 1980, May 26, 51-53.

Zimmerman, S. L. Policy, social policy, and family policy: Concepts, concerns, and analytic tools. *Journal of Marriage and the Family,* 1979, *41*(3), 487-495.

Zimmerman, S. L., Mattessich, P., & Leik, R. Legislators' attitudes toward family policy. *Journal of Marriage and the Family,* 1979, *41*(3), 507-517.

Index